Thomas and the Thomists

Thomas and the Thomists

The Achievement of Thomas Aquinas and His Interpreters

Romanus Cessario, OP, and
Cajetan Cuddy, OP

Fortress Press
Minneapolis

THOMAS AND THE THOMISTS

The Achievement of Thomas Aquinas and His Interpreters

Copyright © 2017 Fortress Press. All rights reserved. Except for brief quotations in critical articles or reviews, no part of this book may be reproduced in any manner without prior written permission from the publisher. Email copyright@fortresspress.com or write to Permissions, Fortress Press, PO Box 1209, Minneapolis, MN 55440-1209.

Cover image: Wikimedia Commons 2016; 1540c Paris plan de la Tapisserie porte St-Jacques by Mbzt

Cover design: Alisha Lofgren

Print ISBN: 978-1-5064-0595-7
eBook ISBN: 978-1-5064-0596-4

This book was produced using Pressbooks.com, and PDF rendering was done by PrinceXML.

For
Benedict M. Ashley, OP
(1915–2013)
and
Guy-Thomas Bedouelle, OP
(1940–2012)
in piam memoriam

Contents

Mapping the Tradition Series ix
Paul Rorem, series advisor

Introduction xi

Part I. Thomas, or A Story of Divine Providence

1. Commencement 3
2. Flourishing 19
3. Denouement 37

Part II. The Thomists, or "The Heritage of Truth"

4. Uneven Beginnings 47
5. Identity and Defense 63
6. Expansion and Recognition 77
7. Catholic Champions 93
8. Sentinels of Truth 109
9. Sound Philosophy for Catholic Doctrine 123

10.	The Actuality of Aquinas and His Commentators	*133*

Select Bibliography *141*

Index *145*

Mapping the Tradition Series

Paul Rorem, series advisor

Mapping the Tradition is a series of brief, compact guides to pivotal thinkers in Christian history. Each volume in this series focuses upon a particular figure, providing a concise but lucid introduction to the central features of each thinker's work and sketching the lasting significance of that thinker for the history of Christian theology.

As well, the series utilizes primary source works from each figure as an entry point for exposition and exploration. Guided by leading scholars in history and theology, primary source texts are reproduced with explanatory commentary and are accompanied by orientational essays on the context, contours, and historical and conceptual legacy of the corpus.

The series is designed for beginning and intermediate students, as well as interested general readers, who will benefit from clear, helpful surveys of thinkers, texts, and theologies from across the epochs of Christian history and introductions to major issues and key historical and intellectual points of development.

Volumes in the series:

Gillian T. W. Ahlgren, *Enkindling Love: The Legacy of Teresa of Avila and John of the Cross*
Romanus Cessario, OP, and Cajetan Cuddy, OP, *Thomas and the Thomists: The Achievements of Thomas Aquinas and His Interpreters*
Paul Rorem, *The Dionysian Mystical Tradition*
Paul R. Sponheim, *Existing Before God: Søren Kierkegaard and the Human Venture*

Forthcoming:

Khaled Anatolios, *Irenaeus of Lyons: The Making of the Great Tradition*
Robert Kolb, *Luther and Christian Freedom*
Andrew Louth, *John of Damascus: The Radiance of Orthodoxy*
John T. Slotemaker, *Anselm of Canterbury and the Search for God*
Terrence N. Tice, *Schleiermacher: The Psychology of Christian Faith and Life*
Thomas G. Weinandy and Daniel A. Keating, *Athanasius: Trinitarian-Incarnational Soteriology and Its Reception*

Introduction

Thomas

Over the centuries, God has ennobled his church with many teachers of "sound doctrine" (2 Tim 4:3). Consider saints and scholars such as Ignatius of Antioch, Irenaeus of Lyons, Ambrose of Milan, Augustine of Hippo, Pseudo-Dionysius, Hugh of Saint-Victor, Bonaventure, Robert Grosseteste, and Henry of Ghent. Each according to his style and abilities has defended and expounded the sound doctrine that the apostle recommended to Timothy. One figure, however, emerges as a favored teacher of evangelically sound doctrine. This honor falls to a Dominican, Friar Thomas Aquinas. While not all students of theology and philosophy may privilege this thirteenth-century theologian, most of them still find themselves obliged to deal with his categories of thought. In short, Thomas Aquinas occupies a high niche in the history of Christian intellectuals. The present volume maps, admittedly with broad strokes, more than seven centuries of the tradition that originates with Aquinas and that has faithfully passed on his sound teachings.

The Catholic Church, to be sure, holds Aquinas in special esteem. It recognizes in his work deep resonances with the deposit of faith, with the authentic tradition. As the nineteenth-century pope Leo XIII strikingly put it:

> Among the Scholastic Doctors, the chief and master of all towers Thomas Aquinas, who, as [Cardinal] Cajetan observes, because "he most venerated the ancient doctors of the Church, in a certain way seems to have inherited the intellect of all."[1]

---

1. Leo XIII, *Aeterni Patris*, no. 17.

The Catholic Church also values Aquinas because he brings forth the new. Again, the same Pope Leo acknowledged that Aquinas's achievement "collected together and cemented, distributed in wonderful order, and so increased with important additions the teachings of his illustrious predecessors."[2] All in all, the Catholic Church recognizes in Aquinas an exemplary realization of what Christ himself says about those learned in divine matters: "Then every scribe who has been instructed in the kingdom of heaven is like the head of a household who brings from his storeroom both the new and the old" (Matt 13:52).

Aquinas wrote during the third quarter of the thirteenth century, so scholastic patterns and pedagogies enrich the Thomist corpus. Historians may mine his works for their own interests. Aquinas, however, surely did not think of his tomes as providing future generations with some prime specimens for diplomatics. He would have been surprised to discover that in some quarters today, his writings are treated like period pieces, that is, medieval texts of mainly historical interest. The church, on the other hand, reveres Aquinas for "the enduring originality" of his thought.[3] Small wonder! Aquinas wrote as a Christian believer. The gospel left him intent upon knowing the truth about reality—and most of all, the truth about the highest reality. A quest for the real drove the man from Roccasecca. The Thomist, in turn, qualifies as a metaphysical realist in the sense that Aquinas's teaching hinges on that which is most formal in being: the *actus essendi* (act of being).[4]

Because of his unique genius, Aquinas still serves as a reliable guide for discovering the truth about reality. He leads the well-disposed student to discover the real truth about real things that originate from the real God. Aquinas knew that only the eternal God could account for the origin and constitution of all that exists. Only being exists in reality. Nonbeing does not exist. This fundamental and somewhat self-evident first principle lies at the heart of Aquinas's philosophical and theological project. No other principle exceeds in importance the real distinction between being and nonbeing. What is more, the human person discovers this principle naturally, through their native powers of knowing. "Our intellect," says Aquinas, "knows being naturally, and whatever essentially belongs to a being as such." Then he adds, "and upon this knowledge is founded the knowledge of first principles, such

---

2. Ibid.
3. John Paul II, *Fides et ratio*, no. 43.
4. See Lawrence Dewan, "St. Thomas and the Distinction between Form and *Esse* in Caused Things," in *Form and Being: Studies in Thomistic Metaphysics* (Washington, DC: Catholic University of America Press, 2006), 188–204.

as the impossibility of simultaneously affirming and denying, and the like."[5] From the real distinction between being and nonbeing, Aquinas went on to discover the real distinction between potency and act. Being is not nothing. However, some beings become something different or even something more. Aquinas remained open to the wisdom of the ancient Greek philosopher Aristotle. The pagan Aristotle was the first to resolve the dispute among those thinkers who could not reconcile their observation of change with the fact of continuity. What happens when the little acorn grows into a big oak tree? Potency, then, is the principle in things that is not nothing, and yet is not act. The real distinction between potency and act, as Aquinas sees it, carries implications for all reality.

With subtlety and insight, Aquinas applied the real distinction between potency and act to matter and form as well as to essence and existence. Matter and essence serve as potential principles. Form and existence serve as actuating principles. All material (and, therefore, created) beings are composed of matter and form. Even pure spiritual intelligences are composed of essence and existence. Aquinas realized that the real distinction between potency and act possessed a universal applicability to all of reality. Since even a substance remains in potency to being further articulated through its accidents or properties, substance and accident are understood in terms of potency and act.[6] In other words, the realism of Thomas Aquinas extends to everything from the minutest subatomic particle to the highest angel. At the same time, the real distinction between potency and act helps the created mind discover something about God himself. God possesses no unactualized capacities; he knows neither materiality nor potentiality. In God alone, according to common teaching, essence and existence remain identical. God receives his existence from no one. His being admits to no further actualization. Simply put, "God is his own existence."[7] Everything else enjoys only borrowed existence.

Guided by his Christian faith, Aquinas perceived depths within the potency and act principle that did not enter the Aristotelian imagination. Though Aristotle recognized that certain objects possess the

---

5. *Summa contra Gentiles* bk. II, c. 83, no. 31. Translation taken from Thomas Aquinas, *Summa Contra Gentiles Book Two: Creation*, trans. James F. Anderson (Notre Dame: University of Notre Dame Press, 1975), 281–82.
6. Here one understands accident as "property" and not the term "accident," to refer to the Aristotelian categories as such.
7. *Summa theologiae* Ia, q. 3, art. 6: "Deus est suum esse." Translation taken from Thomas Aquinas, *Existence and Nature of God*, ed. and trans. Timothy McDermott, vol. 2 (1a. 2–11) of *Summa Theologiae* (London: Blackfriars, 1964), 39.

real capacity to become something different, he did not conceive of the potential of intelligent creatures to become personally united with God. The documents of faith, however, assured Aquinas that they could. Aquinas's realism further serves the Christian religion. The God who creates the intelligible order of reality also reveals his supernatural plan for the universe so that the human mind can grasp it. In Aquinas's view, only a realist philosophy sustains the soteriological realism of Christ's person and work. In his theological writings, at least, Thomas draws from this commonsense principle of being the uncommon sense found in gospel conclusions.

Aquinas, it is true, inhabited the premodern period of Christian thought. He comes before the advent of seventeenth-century empiricist philosophy. An unquenchable appetite for facts and details never dominated Aquinas. He rather sought to understand the reality that underlies the facts of natural and supernatural existence. Likewise, Aquinas antedates post-Cartesian rationalist philosophies and Enlightenment prejudices. For him, philosophical wisdom "explores reality" and does not impose a priori categories on it.[8] In other words, Aquinas was not a theologian of topical specialization or speculative eccentricity. Like the wise persons of the Old Testament, Thomas Aquinas pleaded for wisdom (see Wis 7:7). He sought out principles. From these principles of grace and nature, he developed an exposition of the whole of Christian doctrine. Aquinas was able to distinguish order from chaos, wisdom from foolishness, and grace from nature. One may ask whether Aquinas's providential position in history does not explain "the great merit of [his] giving pride of place to the harmony which exists between faith and reason."[9] In varied ways and according to the exigencies of their circumstances, his followers perpetuate this meritorious legacy.

The Thomists

The suite of Thomist commentators that has flourished over the course of seven centuries testifies to the perennial worth of Thomas Aquinas. Other than Saint Augustine, one stretches to find another Christian theologian who enjoys such a following. Besides, most will agree that those who cite Augustine make up a more diverse group than do the Thomists treated in this volume. Of course, it poses quite a task to

---

8. *Fides et ratio*, no. 44.
9. Ibid., no. 43.

summarize more than seven hundred years of a commentatorial tradition within a textbook designed to introduce readers to Thomas and those who interpret him. In order to give some idea of the dimensions of the Thomist commentatorial tradition, *Thomas and the Thomists* presents a sampling of authors from each of the centuries that follow the death of Aquinas in 1274. This presentation eschews the once customary periodization of the history of Thomist thought. Lexicons, dictionaries, and catalogs afford sufficient evidence to support the claim that the Thomists enjoy a continual presence among religious and philosophical scholars. The argument for continuity among the interpreters of Aquinas does not gainsay the fact that during certain periods and in specific locations, the work of Thomists has received greater support and, therefore, appeared more prominently than in other times and places.

In imitation of their earthly master, Thomists heed Christ's prayer for his disciples: "Consecrate them in the truth. Your word is truth" (John 17:17). In his commentary on this verse of John's Gospel, Aquinas himself explains what animates his authentic followers as they embrace the highest wisdom.

> He [Jesus] says: I have prayed that my disciples be kept from evil; but this is not enough unless they are perfected by what is good: "Depart from evil, and do good" (Ps 37:27). Accordingly he prays, sanctify them, that is, perfect them and make them holy. And do this in the truth, that is, in me, your Son, who am the truth (14:6). It is like saying: Make them share in my perfection and holiness (sanctity). And thus he adds, your word, that is, your Word, is the truth. The meaning is then: Sanctify them in me, the truth, because I, your Word, am the truth.[10]

And again, still commentating on John 17:17, Aquinas offers another reason that applies especially to those who undertake teaching in the church.

> Or, we could say this: Sanctify them, by sending the Holy Spirit. And do this in the truth, that is, in the knowledge of the truths of the faith and of your commandments: "You will know the truth, and the truth will make you free" ([John] 8:32). For we are sanctified by faith and the knowledge of the truth: "the righteousness of God through faith in Jesus Christ for all who believe" (Rom 3:22). He adds, your word is truth, because the truth of God's words is unmixed with falsity: "All the words of my mouth are right-

---

10. Thomas Aquinas, *Commentary on the Gospel of John: Chapters 13-21*, trans. Fabian R. Larcher and James A. Weisheipl (Washington, DC: Catholic University of America Press, 2010), 184, no. 2229.

eous; there is nothing twisted or crooked in them" (Prov 8:8). Further, his word teaches the uncreated truth.[11]

While other Christian thinkers may seek uncreated truth, those who follow and interpret Aquinas faithfully commit themselves to the project as an ecclesial vocation. They accept that the theologian's "role is to pursue in a particular way an ever deeper understanding of the Word of God found in the inspired Scriptures and handed on by the living Tradition of the Church ... in communion with the Magisterium which has been charged with the responsibility of preserving the deposit of faith."[12] Thomists, therefore, regard critically those philosophical movements that hamper them in this, their privileged pursuit of truth.

Some scholars prefer to approach the Thomist commentatorial tradition as a loose series of diachronic intellectual exercises.[13] Others choose to examine the writings of the Thomists through a hermeneutic lens of politics—ecclesial, intellectual, or both.[14] It would be wrong, however, to regard the Thomists included in this overview as random figures engrossed in tedious and long-forgotten intellectual exchanges. The present work, rather, provides an account of men and women engaged in the living search for truth. Thomists put both theology and philosophy at the service of the church's mission to evangelize the nations, the Great Commission (see Matt 28:18–20). It should come as no surprise, then, to discover that the majority of Thomists considered within this volume have belonged to the institutes of consecrated life that flourish within the church. These persons enjoy a privileged starting point on the road toward developing a sanctified intelligence for service to the church's ministry. Most Thomists, whether clerics or lay, worked during periods dominated by intellectual conflicts of all kinds. Each, however, shared the same commitment to the truth of things that Aquinas passionately embraced. All Thomists sought wisdom, though without unnecessary accommodation to the intellectual fashion of their day. They also share Aquinas's conviction that one's humanity, academic achievement, and personal sanctity work together in the search for truth. Blind party allegiance does not suffice to join

---

11. Ibid., 184–85.
12. Congregation for the Doctrine of the Faith, 1990 Instruction, *Donum Veritatis*, On the Ecclesial Vocation of the Theologian, no. 6.
13. See, for example, Gerald Vann, *Saint Thomas Aquinas* (New York: Benziger Brothers, 1940), 70.
14. For example, see James Hennesey, "Leo XIII's Thomistic Revival: A Political and Philosophical Event," *Journal of Religion* 58 Supplement (1978): S185–97.

the Thomist band; likewise, neither does the possession of academic distinctions.

Students of Aquinas do not simply repeat the utterances of their master. Rather, they receive the essential philosophical and theological principles from the Angelic Doctor and then apply these sound principles to the unique questions, challenges, and requirements that their own period raises. Thomists do not concur on every detail of the philosophy or theology that they produce. This comes as no surprise when we consider the different cultures and diverse questions that have inspired the work of Aquinas's students. Discrepancies among Thomists usually find their explanations from within the authors' historical contexts. For example, Cardinal Cajetan engaged in the sixteenth century the specific objections to Thomist thought posed by earlier thinkers such as Durandus and Duns Scotus. Later, Dominic Báñez responded to the questions raised by the Protestant reformer and self-admitted theological innovator Luis de Molina. In the seventeenth century, John of St. Thomas interacted with the figures of early modern thought and identified the eclectic approaches of theologians whose thinking originates elsewhere than Aquinas's does. Take a step back to the fourteenth century, and we find that even Catherine of Siena resonates with the real distinction when she reports that the Eternal Father addressed her saying, "You are she who is not; I AM HE WHO IS."[15]

Contemporary students of Christian doctrine face many circumstances that did not mark the intellectual cultures of earlier centuries. However, like Aquinas and his interpreters, today's students of theology can expect to discover sapiential clarity when they approach their discipline under the guidance of ungainsayable principles. Like every introductory text, this volume will have achieved its purpose to the extent that it encourages students to continue their exploration into the thought of Thomas Aquinas and of the authentic interpretative tradition that has cultivated the fruit of his enduring originality for more than seven centuries.

---

15. Raymond of Capua, *The Life of Catherine of Siena*, trans. Conleth Kearns (Wilmington, DE: Michael Glazier, 1980), 91.

PART I

Thomas, or A Story of Divine Providence

1
―

Commencement

Providential Advantage

As Shakespeare has engraved on the educated Western memory, English longbow archers overcame, against all odds, their French crossbow counterparts when the respective warring armies engaged near the chateau of Agincourt on Saint Crispin's Day, 25 October 1415.[1] Some 160 years earlier, the French royal archers had met another challenge, but that time they did so successfully. They guarded, in 1256, the Dominican priory of Saint-Jacques against local Parisian street brawlers who resented the arrival of a new class of teachers drawn from a group of recently instituted mendicant orders like the Dominicans. Today, tourists in Paris may visit the Pantheon, located at the top of the Rue Soufflot. As they move up this ascending street from the boulevard Saint-Michel, they pass close by the location of the now demolished medieval priory whose list of celebrated inhabitants includes the theologian and philosopher Thomas Aquinas (1224/25–1274).[2] He would become the first saint after the close of the patristic period the pope, in 1568, officially recognized as a doctor of the church.[3] In spring

---

1. William Shakespeare, *Henry V*, act 4, scene 3.
2. For an informative overview of the history of this convent, see Barbara Beaumont and Guy Bedouelle, *Guide des Lieux Dominicains: France, Belgique sud, Suisse romande* (Paris: Edition Horay, 2004), 122–23.
3. See Nicole Lemaître, *Saint Pie V* (Paris: Fayard, 1994), 168.

1256, however, this young priest was just starting out in his university career. The French king Louis IX, with the help of his archers, ensured that an unruly mob would not impede the Dominican master of theology from finishing his course of lectures. Though he benefitted from the royal support, Aquinas was not born cosmopolitan French. His earthly life began in a feudal setting on the Italian peninsula.

The Latium (Lazio) region of middle Italy, with its capital at Rome, probably owes its name to the flat and rolling landscape (*latus*) that even today enables this region to serve as an agricultural center—a *terroir*—for wine grapes, fruit, vegetables, and olives. The region also gives us the English word *Latin* after its occupants, the Latini or the Latins. Here, at an elevated, craggy place called Roccasecca, Thomas Aquinas was born around the first quarter of the thirteenth century.[4] His early education benefitted from the proximity of his birthplace to the epicenter of Western monasticism, the Abbey of Montecassino. Under the tutelage of the monks of Saint Benedict, whose sepulcher lies under the abbey's church, the young nobleman grew into early manhood. One recognized scholar, Martin Grabmann, has observed how a sense of peace characterizes Aquinas's person and writings. Grabmann accounts for this quality by appealing to the *Pax* that Saint Benedict established as the motto for his monasteries. Each monastery is meant to embody Saint Augustine's vision of peace: *pax est tranquillitas ordinis* (peace is the tranquility resulting from order).[5] The rhythms of the monastic life as prescribed in the *Rule of Saint Benedict* left their mark on the teenaged Thomas Aquinas, even after various circumstances of his early history conspired to bring him to Naples in pursuit of higher studies.

Once he arrived in the metropolitan center of Naples, the young man from Roccasecca, who because of his family lineage enjoyed social standing, came under the influence of another master of consecrated religious life, the Spaniard Dominic de Guzman (d. 1221). The Order of Preachers, or Dominicans, as its members are commonly known, arrived in Naples shortly after Frederick II Hohenstaufen, the Holy Roman emperor, founded a university there in 1224. A series of charm-

---

4. Biographical and other historical details concerning the life of Thomas Aquinas depend on the major and latest authoritative biography by Jean-Pierre Torrell, *Saint Thomas Aquinas*, vol. 1, *The Person and His Work*, trans. Robert Royal, rev. ed. (Washington, DC: Catholic University of America Press, 2005).
5. Martin Grabmann, *The Interior Life of St. Thomas Aquinas: Presented from His Works and the Acts of His Canonization Process*, trans. Nicholas Ashenbrener (Milwaukee, WI: Bruce Publishing, 1951), 50–52. The reference occurs in Saint Augustine, *The City of God*, 19.13, where the author writes "pax omnium rerum tranquillitas ordinis."

ing incidents narrated in the biography of Aquinas, which includes his stealthy escape from confinement in a family castle, testify to the upset that arises when a son of privilege departs from centuries-old social conventions and seeks instead to espouse a way of service to a church that had received papal recognition only in 1216. Of course, God himself establishes the actual order from which the tranquillity of any given moment arises. The young Thomas Aquinas discovered this truth about how God works decades before he affirmed it in his *Summa theologiae*: "The effect of divine Providence is for a thing to come about not just anyhow but in its own proper style, necessarily or contingently as the case may be."[6] At Naples, and despite some expression of familial opposition, Thomas Aquinas received the black and white habit that Saint Dominic had bequeathed to his friars. The newly minted Fra Tommaso—or its equivalent in the Neapolitan dialect of the day—immediately took up the distinctive rhythms of the Dominican convent, or priory, where older monastic practices were adapted to suit the Order's apostolic form of life.

Thomas Aquinas chose a form of religious commitment that would allow him to engage in the intellectual life as a properly evangelical or missionary enterprise. He later elaborated three reasons why a religious institute may include serious study among its characteristic works.[7] First, study aids contemplation by directing a person's mind to sacred things and, indirectly, by removing erroneous notions about divine things. Second, study proves indispensable for the preaching office that is ordered to address human intelligence. Aquinas gives the example of Saint Paul, who stipulates to Titus that "a bishop . . . will be able both to exhort with sound doctrine and refute opponents" (Titus 1:7–9). Third, the habit of study abets one's following of the evangelical counsels of chastity, poverty, and obedience. Study, on Aquinas's testimony, turns the mind toward noble thoughts and so away from prurient interests, eases the desire for material goods as long as a man finds his wealth in texts, and prompts obedience to the extent that study exposes the attractiveness of sacred truth.

Today, we have become accustomed to Catholic religious institutes that carry out educational missions. In the thirteenth century, however, it was novel for a religious institute or order to include study

---

6. *Summa theologiae* 1a, q. 22, art. 4, ad 1. Translation taken from Thomas Aquinas, *God's Will and Providence*, ed. and trans. Thomas Gilby, introduction and appendix by Ian Hislop, vol. 5 (1a. 19–26) of *Summa Theologiae* (London: Blackfriars, 1967), 103.
7. See *Summa theologiae* 2a–2ae, q. 188, art. 5.

among its means of sanctification. Once Thomas Aquinas committed himself to the Order of Friars Preachers, the university and classroom became his usual place of assignment and his preferred field of apostolic engagement.[8] Before he could take up the Dominican mission, however, Aquinas first required Dominican intellectual formation. Completion of the course of institutional or basic studies brought the young Thomas Aquinas to Paris and afterward to Cologne. This onetime Roman colony (*Colonia*) welcomed both Aquinas and his teacher, the German Dominican Albert, called the Great on account of his extensive learning. Albert was sent to Cologne in order to set up a school for Dominican students.[9] Though the magnificent Gothic cathedral that today dominates the Cologne skyline was still in the initial phases of construction, the city housed from the mid-tenth century one of the seven electors of the Holy Roman Empire. The Rhineland city therefore enjoyed political standing. Aquinas completed what effectively comprised his seminary studies at Cologne. In all likelihood, he received priestly ordination there as well.

Ordering Wisdom

The church has always associated the priesthood with learning, even though clerics enjoyed better educations at different periods in her two-millennium history than they did at others. "Knowledge of the Law," Aquinas remarked about the Old Testament priesthood, "was so closely bound up with the priestly office that being charged with the office meant being charged with the Law."[10] While the Christian priesthood remains ordered principally to enacting the eucharistic sacrifice, the exercise of the priesthood of Jesus Christ entails as an essential constitutive responsibility, a *munus*, the teaching office that Christ confides to his apostles.[11] When Aquinas, in his *Summa theologiae*, inquires whether Christ should have written a book, he raises the issue of

---

8. For a convenient collection of texts where Aquinas treats those religious who teach and preach, see Caesarius Nalpathamkalam, "Teaching and Preaching Orders according to St. Thomas Aquinas," *Laval théologique et philosophique* 23, no. 2 (1967): 269–305.
9. For information on this important figure in the history of Western thought, see James A. Weisheipl, "The Life and Works of St. Albert the Great," in *Albertus Magnus and the Sciences: Commemorative Essays, 1980*, ed. James A. Weisheipl (Toronto: Pontifical Institute of Mediaeval Studies, 1980), 13–52.
10. *Summa theologiae* 2a–2ae, q. 16, art. 2, ad 3. Translation taken from Thomas Aquinas, *Consequences of Faith*, ed. and trans. Thomas Gilby, vol. 32 (2a2ae. 8–16) of *Summa Theologiae* (London: Blackfriars, 1975), 153.
11. For Aquinas's views on the priesthood and the Eucharist, see *Summa theologiae* 3a, q. 67, art. 2. See also, *Summa theologiae* 2a–2ae, q. 177, art. 2: "to teach and persuade publically in Church is not the task of subjects but of prelates." Translation taken from Thomas Aquinas, *Prophecy and other*

priestly learning and exposes its importance for the right exercise of the teaching office.[12] His argument turns on the desired orderliness that Christ intends to control the dissemination of his gospel. Had Christ written a book, Aquinas conjectures, his teaching would have reached everyone immediately. Instead, Christ wished that his teaching would indeed reach everyone but in an ordered and mediated manner. Christ taught his disciples immediately, and they in turn passed on his teaching to succeeding generations—a process we today call evangelization. Priests, in other words, are to teach as if they are Christ's living book. Their teaching office, exercised faithfully throughout the ages, ensures that each generation will receive the catholic and apostolic faith. Of course, to accomplish this mission, all priests must undertake prolonged study in order to prepare themselves to exercise well their teaching office. Although the connection today goes frequently unnoticed, Aquinas's priesthood shaped his approach to the study of sacred truth. This son of privilege so cherished his participation in the providential ordering that governs the communication of divine truth that he flatly refused forms of ecclesiastical preferment to which, according to the customs of the day, his family's rank would have entitled him. Pope Clement IV, for example, offered Aquinas the archbishopric of Naples, but he declined it (*sed recusavit recipere*).[13]

Aquinas developed from his earliest years an appreciation for the orderly conduct of all human affairs. The political order of his Italian peninsula homeland (contested in his day between Holy Roman emperor and pope), the monastic order observed at Montecassino, and the conventual order sustained by Aquinas and his fellow Dominicans—each of these life experiences left its mark on the mind and personality of this young Italian friar. In fact, for nearly 750 years, the works of Aquinas that have been most read and useful to those doing Catholic theology are the treatises where he manifestly introduces an intelligible order—not to be confused with encyclopedic organization—into his theological materials. To appreciate Aquinas's achievement, one need only attend to the pedagogical shortcomings of the early medieval etymologies, glosses, florilegia, sermons, and so forth that supplied into the twelfth century materials for Christian instruction. These unwieldy collections, even when organized around letters

---

Charisms, ed. and trans. Roland Potter, vol. 45 (2a2ae. 171–78) of *Summa Theologiae* (London: Blackfriars, 1970), 133.

12. See *Summa theologiae* 3a, q. 42, art. 4.
13. See Tolomeo di Lucca, *Historia ecclesiastica nova*, 22.39, in *S. Thomae Aquinatis vitae fontes praecipuae*, ed. Angelico Ferrua (Alba: Edizioni Domenicane, 1968), 360.

of the alphabet or verses of Scripture, often served more to edify than instruct. The young Aquinas surely discovered firsthand the benefits of an orderly presentation of divine truth when he sat in the classroom of Albertus Magnus (ca. 1200–1280).[14] Trustworthy medieval legends recount that as Albert discovered the natural gifts of mind that his corpulent Italian student displayed, he prophesied the place that Aquinas would, in fact, attain in the church: "We call him the dumb ox, but he will make resound in his doctrine such a bellowing that it will echo throughout the whole world."[15] As it turns out, Albert the Great was spot on.

Some scholars suggest that during his time spent studying in Cologne, Aquinas began the practice of commenting on the sacred Scriptures. If so, then Aquinas, who may have functioned like a graduate assistant for Master Albert, would have devoted his first effort at composing a scriptural annotation on the book of Isaiah, the Old Testament prophet cherished for his heralding of the Messiah.[16] During the course of his Dominican life, Aquinas returned frequently to the exposition of sacred Scripture. It is said that his last composition also followed an Old Testament theme, although no manuscript trace remains.[17] While on his deathbed, so the story goes, Aquinas explained to attentive monks the spiritual meaning of the Song of Songs, the haunting love song that, more than a century before, had inspired the bridal mysticism of Bernard of Clairvaux (d. 1153). All in all, scholars attribute some eleven biblical commentaries, expositions, glosses, and annotations to the pen of Thomas Aquinas.[18] These texts do not represent the private spiritual notebooks of a professional teacher. The study of sacred Scripture formed an integral part of Aquinas's intellectual project, which, as his teaching developed, would progress far

---

14. For a still useful account of the development of theological science as it emerges in the twelfth century, see M.-D. Chenu, *Nature, Man, and Society in the Twelfth Century: Essays on New Theological Perspectives in the Latin West*, ed. and trans. Jerome Taylor and Lester K. Little (Chicago: University of Chicago Press, 1968), especially chap. 8, 270–309.
15. Jean-Pierre Torrell, *Aquinas's Summa: Background, Structure, and Reception*, trans. Benedict M. Guevin (Washington, DC: Catholic University of America Press, 2005), 26. Other ancient sources say that "ox" refers to the corpulence and beauty of Aquinas's physical stature.
16. See *Summa theologiae* 2a–2ae, q. 2, art. 7, ad 2. Also see James A. Weisheipl, *Friar Thomas D'Aquino: His Life, Thought, and Works* (Washington, DC: Catholic University of America Press, 1983), 45. For further information on this early biblical writing, see Jean-Pierre Torrell and Denise Bouthillier, "Quand saint Thomas méditait sur le prophète Isaïe," *Revue Thomiste* 90, no. 1 (1990): 5–47.
17. Weisheipl, *Friar Thomas D'Aquino*, 369.
18. See G. Emery, "Brief Catalogue of the Works of Saint Thomas Aquinas," in *Saint Thomas Aquinas*, vol. 1, *The Person and his Work*, by Jean-Pierre Torrell, rev. ed. (Washington, DC: Catholic University of America Press, 2005), 337–41.

beyond the mode of both scriptural commentary and its basic exposition, the postil.

The start of the school year in 1252 found Aquinas back in Paris, which one keen contemporary observer described as "the oven where the intellectual bread of the Latin world was baked."[19] There, Aquinas began his formal teaching career under the guidance of a senior Dominican, Elias Brunet. As one of his major systematic works bears witness, Aquinas began his teaching career by commenting on the *Sentences* of Peter Lombard, a scholar who became bishop of Paris (where he died about 1160).[20] University practice stipulated that young professors produce a written commentary on this standard encyclopedia of Catholic theology that dates back to the middle of the twelfth century (1155–1158). For the medieval theologian, the production of a *Sentence* commentary may be compared roughly to the contemporary scholar's completion of a doctoral dissertation. It is difficult to overestimate the influence that the *Four Books of the Sentences* has exercised on the history of teaching Catholic theology. Commentaries on the *Sentences* were "the most important sources of systematic theology . . . well into the sixteenth century."[21] Indeed, new commentaries appeared into the seventeenth century—for example, that of Juan Martinez de Ripalda (d. 1648). Even the first major commentator on Aquinas himself, John Capreolus (1380–1444), followed the order of the *Sentences* in his thoroughly Thomistic *Defensiones*.[22] Further, the systematic presentation of Catholic doctrine devised by Lombard still provides the prototype for a thoroughgoing study of Catholic doctrine. According to the official instructions provided today by the Catholic Church, standard curricula in Catholic theology schools must include the topics distinguished by Lombard in his *Sentences*.

During the 1250s, the tasks of commenting and teaching the *Sentences* were considered prefatory to one's full integration into the professorial corps. As the above-mentioned protection service by the royal archers suggests, the circumstances in Paris for the Dominicans and other mendicant friars, such as the followers of Francis of Assisi, were not favorable to the peaceful carrying out of their university work. The

---

19. See M.-D. Chenu, *Aquinas and His Role in Theology*, trans. Paul Philibert (Collegeville, MN: Liturgical Press, 2002), 18.
20. For further information on the *Sententiae in IV libros distinctae*, see Ulrich G. Leinsle, *Introduction to Scholastic Theology*, trans. Michael J. Miller (Washington, DC: Catholic University of America Press, 2010), 98–102.
21. Ibid., 99.
22. See John Capreolus, *On the Virtues*, ed. and trans. Kevin White and Romanus Cessario (Washington, DC: Catholic University of America Press, 2001).

controversy that required the royal protection services also merited an intervention by the pope, who requested that, even in view of the public opposition, the university authorities promote Thomas Aquinas into its corps of professors. This meant that he would have to prepare and deliver an inaugural lecture, called a *principium* (a starting point), in which the new master would exhibit his comprehensive and architectonic grasp of the theological materials. Though barely thirty years of age, Aquinas rose to the challenge. This does not mean that he avoided the normal anxieties that such an exercise would generate in a beginner. Fortunately, heavenly assistance arrived in a somewhat miraculous manner. Aquinas later confided to several of his companions that in answer to his prayers for help in choosing a proper theme for his lecture, a venerable Dominican appeared to him while he was sleeping one night and indicated a specific psalm on which he was to speak.

The celestial visitor, whom the tradition identifies as Saint Dominic himself, selected a verse of Psalms that Dominicans would have sung as part of their weekly choral recitation of the psalter. Psalm 104:13 runs in part as follows: "Rigans montes de superioribus suis de fructu operum tuorum satiabitur terra" (You water the mountains from your palace; by your labor the earth abounds). The mention of "from on high" (*de superioribus*) suggests to Aquinas that the theologian should look heavenward for the principle of all that exists and for the source of the wisdom required to talk about it. Aquinas makes his general theme clear in the first words of his inaugural lecture by drawing a comparison between natural rainfall and the illuminations that flow from God.

> It is plain to the senses that from the highest clouds rain flows forth by which the mountains and rivers are refreshed and send themselves forth so that the satiated earth can bear fruit. Similarly, from the heights of divine wisdom the minds of the learned, represented by the mountains, are watered, by whose ministry the light of divine wisdom reached to the minds of those who listen.[23]

At the very start of his career, Aquinas directs attention to the unity that characterizes the theological science and, further, to the unity of truth itself. The various mediations that come into play in the communication of divine truth, including the canonical Scriptures, do not entail its breakup or fragmentation.[24] As his *principium, Rigans montes*,

---

23. "On the Commendation of Sacred Scripture," in *Thomas Aquinas: Selected Writings*, ed. and trans. Ralph McInerny (New York: Penguin Books, 1998), 13.

goes on to explain, God bestows a sharing in divine wisdom through a multiplicity of mediations, each of which remains bound to the one divine wisdom that governs "on high" all that exists. For much of contemporary theology, Aquinas's *principium* finds itself "more honor'd in the breach than the observance."[25]

In his *principium*, whose overall theme includes how a teacher should give instruction in matters of divinity, Aquinas explains the three reasons that warrant placing the holy teaching that flows from God in the "heights."[26] First, the origin of theology, which is the divine wisdom itself. Second, the subtlety of matter that it treats. Third, the sublimity of the end or completion unto which the holy teaching (*sacra doctrina*) ushers those who receive it.[27] His explanation of the origins of the holy teaching that God confides to Christ and his church leads Aquinas next to speak about the qualities of those who teach and preach this (to use Aquinas's own expression) *sacra doctrina*. He ends his discourse by stipulating the qualities to be desired in those who wish to receive fruitfully the *sacra doctrina*. Today, we would easily describe an inaugural lecture of this kind as programmatic. *Rigans montes*, which was delivered under the protection of the royal archers, sets a trajectory, much like the archer himself who fixes his bow at a target. Aquinas was familiar with the use of arrows.[28] In his magisterial *principium*, we find indicated the seminal reason for the unity and purpose both of Aquinas's speculative work and of the commentatorial tradition that follows upon it. For Aquinas and those who follow him, theologians create an organic structure for explicating the content of divine truth. It reveals a wisdom that appears at once both contemplative and active. In each of these moments, the practitioners of *sacra doctrina*—theologians broadly construed—draw upon God's knowledge of himself even as they aim to lead themselves and others by means of this lofty teaching back toward God. What holds for the order of grace also holds for the order of nature.

---

24. For an illuminating account of this Thomist insight, see Francisco P. Muñiz, *The Work of Theology*, trans. John P. Reid (Washington, DC: Thomist Press, 1953).
25. William Shakespeare, *Hamlet*, act 1, scene 4, line 18.
26. In Aquinas's lapidary Latin formulation: "Habet enim sacra doctrina altitudinem ex tribus."
27. For Aquinas's own treatment of the *sacra doctrina*, see *Summa theologiae* 1a, q. 1. Considerable literature aims to expound on this subject; for one neglected study, see Thomas C. O'Brien, "'Sacra Doctrina' Revisited: The Context of Medieval Education," *The Thomist* 41, no. 4 (1977): 475–509.
28. See Thomas Aquinas, *The Literal Exposition on Job: A Scriptural Commentary Concerning Providence*, trans. Anthony Damico (Atlanta: Scholars Press, 1989), 466: "A man also attacks from a distance with arrows and the stones of a sling" (*Impugnat etiam homo a remotis per sagittas et lapides fundae*). For further discussion of Aquinas's knowledge of weapons, see Edward A. Synan, "St. Thomas Aquinas and the Profession of Arms," *Mediaeval Studies* 50, no. 1 (1988): 404–37.

In the twentieth century, one of Aquinas's best modern commentators took up the theme of principle when he examined the conception of philosophical truth that animates Aquinas's vast intellectual achievement. Reginald Garrigou-Lagrange, OP, has pointed out that "the definition of potency determines the Thomistic synthesis."[29] The real distinction between potency and act serves as the heart of Saint Thomas's speculative legacy. Potency only exists in relation to some actuality. And limited act only exists because of he who is pure act. When Aquinas inquires whether God is truth, he returns to the principle that essence and existence are identical in God. Pure act—essence that is existence—alone abides as the supreme and original truth. "For his being is not only in conformity with his intellect, but is his very act of knowing; and his act of knowing is the measure and cause of all other being and all other intellect; and he himself is his own being and his own act of knowing."[30] The argument may appear dense, but the reality proves simple to grasp. God measures all things even though he remains unmeasured by anything. God is pure act; God is truth.

Aquinas, even at this early stage in his career, privileges the orderly communication of divine truth to the world by a God who speaks to his creatures. The apostle of truth first beholds God through loving contemplation in order to communicate the Highest Truth effectively. Christian allegorical interpretation of the Bible finds this plan of divine wisdom illustrated in the account of Jacob's Ladder where angels are seen "going up and down on it" (Gen 28:12). For example, Saint Caesarius of Arles (d. 542) taught that the angels represent apostles and teachers who ascend to the perfect when they preach and descend to the simple when they offer instruction.[31] Aquinas complements this teaching with the assertion that the biblical patriarchs, even before the Mosaic law, performed acts of true religion inasmuch as their offerings, sacrifices, and holocausts "profess their worship of God as the beginning and end of all."[32]

In *Rigans montes*, Aquinas teaches that the dependency of the creature on God reaches back to creation's deepest origin, its existence, and

---

29. Reginald Garrigou-Lagrange, *Reality: A Synthesis of Thomistic Thought*, trans. Patrick Cummins (St. Louis: Herder, 1950), 37.
30. *Summa theologiae* 1a, q. 16, art. 5. Translation taken from Thomas Aquinas, *Knowledge in God*, ed. and trans. Thomas Gornall, vol. 4 (1a. 14–18) of *Summa Theologiae* (London: Blackfriars, 1964), 89.
31. "Sermo LXXXVII: De Scala Iacob," in *Sancti Caesarii Arelatensis Sermones*, ed. Germain Morin, Corpus Christianorum, Series Latina, vol. 103 (Turnhout: Brepols, 1953), 357–61.
32. *Summa theologiae* 1a-2ae, q. 103, art. 1, ad 1. Translation taken from Thomas Aquinas, *The Old Law*, ed. and trans. David Bourke and Arthur Littledale, vol. 29 (1a2ae. 98–105) of *Summa Theologiae* (London: Blackfriars, 1969), 233.

extends to include everything that is knowable by creatures. Creation finds its perfection to the extent that it corresponds to the truth that measures all things. Of course, only the intelligent creature can choose to act against the truth. The breathtaking compass of this inaugural lesson owes something to Aquinas's early training with the Benedictine monks. While still a young boy in the cloister of Montecassino, Aquinas found there a living example of the peace that order infuses into the rhythms of everyday life. Later, while a student with the Dominicans, he discovered another manifestation of order that informs the studious acquisition of truth.

As suggested above, the Dominican way of life, which Aquinas chose less than a quarter-century after the founder died, favors the acquisition of sacred truth by the distinctive way that it combines assiduous study with the exercises that one associates with monastic life, especially the following of the evangelical counsels and the common praying of the Liturgy of the Hours. His espousal of truth and peace disposes Aquinas to discover and to appreciate, profoundly, the sapiential order of the divine science. The entrance antiphon for the Mass celebrated on 28 January, his current feast day, captures this theme: "In the midst of the Church he opened his mouth, and the Lord filled him with the spirit of wisdom and understanding and clothed him in a robe of glory."[33] Eighteen years of life remained for the man from Roccasecca to develop the implications of a principle that remains unfathomable except to God.

The Skilled Archer

The medieval teaching office required three exercises by a professor in order to fulfill his professional responsibilities. By the time Aquinas joined the ranks of university masters, these obligations had become captured in the Latin triplet: *legere, disputare, praedicare*. First, the master must read (*legere*), which commits him mainly to read and to analyze the Bible. By the time Aquinas began in the mid-thirteenth century, professorial reading also included expositing other literature, such as the works of Aristotle, which had become available in Latin from various sources and, in all but a few cases, were translated directly from the Greek.[34]

---

33. The ancient Latin text adapts the words of Sirach 15:5: "In medio Ecclesiae aperuit os eius, et implevit eum Dominus spiritu sapientiae et intellectus; stolam gloriae induit eum."
34. See appendix B in *The Cambridge History of Medieval Philosophy*, vol. 1, ed. Robert Pasnau (Cambridge: Cambridge University Press, 2009), 793–97.

Second, the master must be able to hold his own in public debates, to dispute with others (*disputare*). Disputation unfolds as an exercise in discursive argumentation. The disputation does not concern the engagement of conflicting parties, such as when one disputes a charge on a credit account. Disputation, rather, provides a way for learned men to explore different points of view with an eye toward reaching, at the end of strictly controlled exchanges, a determination or conclusion about the matter under disputation. Alasdair MacIntyre speaks about a "constrained disagreement" that characterizes Aquinas's theological method.[35] Aquinas devoted considerable time to engaging in disputations, which for the medieval university world would have satisfied the same intellectual appetites that in the twenty-first century are sated by televised debates, bloggers, and talk shows (where what is said appears to be anything but constrained). Of course, the medieval disputations limited themselves to the discussion of serious topics in the sacred sciences, about which scholars and students nonetheless entertained a wide variety of opinions. Disputation, whether held privately (that is, between the master and his students) or publicly (that is, open to the general university audience), provided a forum for teaching. The unit of instruction is known as a *quaestio*, that is, a question that is put up for discussion. However, scholars disagree about how Aquinas's eight printed disputations, his disputed questions (*quaestiones disputatae*), correspond to the individual teaching sessions that Aquinas undertook during his academic tenures.

Lastly, *praedicare* (preaching) fell among the medieval master's main obligations. It is generally agreed that the religious exercise of preaching, which required a man's having received the sacrament of holy orders, was associated with the medieval educational project in a way that would surprise the habitués of the modern secular university, even those who may still engage a university preacher. Preaching in a church was considered professorial inasmuch as pulpit preaching supplied the preferred venue for the communication of divine truth. This arrangement did not arise from a spirit of elitism. Rather, it was generally thought that the preacher's authority should not be compromised by his ignorance.

Aquinas applied himself to these professional responsibilities, as did the other university masters. Although the fact often passes without notice, Aquinas fulfilled his charge while living under the rule of

---

35. Alasdair MacIntyre, *Three Rival Versions of Moral Enquiry: Encyclopedia, Genealogy, and Tradition* (Notre Dame: University of Notre Dame Press, 1990), 233.

French monarchs. For his part, King Louis IX favored the Dominicans with major benefactions that allowed them to construct the buildings that sheltered Aquinas during his first Parisian regency, a term reserved to describe a master functioning in an official university post, and again during his second.

The positioning of the royal archers before the Dominican priory of Saint-Jacques came about not only to ensure crowd control. The rabble-rousers represented the public face of some serious challenges to the legitimacy of the new mendicant orders operating within a university setting. The Catholic clergy exists in two forms of service to the church. One group owes its allegiance to the local bishop and serves the pastoral needs of the local church; the other group (monks, friars, etc.) populates the various religious institutes that have developed over the course of the centuries. One factor that remains relevant to what are known as the anti-mendicant quarrels concerns the difference in financial arrangements that exists between the two groups. Secular priests and clerics manage their own financial resources and retain the capacity to own property, whereas the monk or religious makes a vow of poverty within the context of a common life and so forgoes the right to hold possessions as his own. By the middle of the thirteenth century, not everyone in Paris understood that the newly formed mendicant (from the Latin for begging, *mendicare*) orders proposed to make their living by seeking alms. This provision for daily living represents a departure from the way that the older monastic orders met their needs. Monks, according to the emblematic injunction of Saint Benedict, *Ora et Labora*, divided their time between prayer and work. The latter was meant to produce revenue in order to support the monastic community.

One should also recall, as M.-D. Chenu has pointed out, that the medieval university was stamped with an ecclesiastical character such that all of its resources "were dependent on a regime of clerics."[36] No wonder the clerics who did not belong to religious orders—namely, the secular masters who earned their living as professors at the University of Paris—wondered why the new institutes of mendicant friars began to occupy some of the positions that traditionally had been reserved for them. Why, these secular clerics must have asked, did the mendicants not support themselves like the monks through manual labor? This bewilderment, fueled by a certain resentment, explains Aquinas's

---

36. M.-D. Chenu, *Toward Understanding Saint Thomas*, trans. A. M. Landry and D. Hughes (Chicago: Henry Regnery Publishing, 1964), 18.

concern for giving clear reasons as to why a religious institute could legitimately devote itself to the study of sacred truth and, at the same time, request the alms of the Christian faithful in order to support its way of life. Other factors such as prestige and influence in civil society also entered into the dissatisfaction that some of the secular masters allowed to fester into open opposition. At the center of the 1250s controversy stands the figure of a secular cleric named William of Saint-Amour, whose Luddite opinions were rejected flatly by the pope. Aquinas answered the specious arguments found in William's inflammatory rhetoric with his own impassioned treatise, *Contra impugnantes Dei cultum et religionem* (Against Those Who Attack Religion and the Worship of God).[37] The conflict eventually reached a truce, though not a settlement. During his second teaching stint, or regency, at Paris, Thomas Aquinas would face another round of anti-mendicant opposition.

G. K. Chesterton has called the Paris of Aquinas's day "a Sunrise in the North." The British author imagines that "the new Paris ultimately left behind by St. Louis must have been a thing white like lilies and splendid as the oriflamme."[38] Chesterton goes on to observe that the style of the Gothic period, when newly constructed, must have seemed like "a new flight of architecture, as startling as flying-ships."[39] From what we can infer, however, Thomas Aquinas was not taken by the splendors of the medieval City of Lights. Once, when he and his students were returning to Paris, his students remarked on its splendor, and one of them asked whether Aquinas would enjoy being its lord.[40] Aquinas answered, in the paraphrase of Chesterton, "I would rather have that Chrysostom MS. I can't get hold of."[41]

In keeping with his commitment to the study of the sacred sciences, Saint Dominic sent his first followers to study at Paris, and he himself established foundations in other university towns of Europe: Bologna, Palencia, Montpellier, and Oxford.[42] This affinity for university placements explains the Dominican practice that prescribed a swift rotation

---

37. For further information, see the scholarly study by Mary C. Sommers, "Defense and Discovery: Brother Thomas's *Contra impugnantes*," in *Laudemus viros gloriosos: Essays in Honor of Armand Maurer, CSB*, ed. R. E. Houser (Notre Dame: University of Notre Dame Press, 2007), 184–208.
38. G. K. Chesterton, *Saint Thomas Aquinas* (San Francisco: Ignatius Press, 2002), 92–93.
39. Ibid., 93.
40. See Weisheipl, *Friar Thomas D'Aquino*, 121.
41. Chesterton, *Saint Thomas Aquinas*, 93.
42. For further discussion, see Benedict M. Ashley, *The Dominicans* (Collegeville, MN: Liturgical Press, 1990), 29. Montpellier had, in fact, been a university town since the second half of the twelfth century, although Pope Nicholas IV gave the faculties university status only in 1289.

of masters in and out of the regency periods at Paris. The procedure allowed the Order to obtain credentials for as many of its members as possible and, after the completion of a three-year term at Paris, to send the newly minted masters to other university cities where the Order of Saint Dominic, following the example of its founder, continued to establish its priories. Thomas Aquinas followed this pattern of service, and after the completion of his triennium, left Paris for another assignment. Shortly before his departure, however, he attended a general chapter, the supreme legislative body for the Dominican Order, which was held at Valenciennes in northern France.

His attendance at this meeting resulted in Aquinas's giving shape to a plan that would ensure the proper intellectual formation of future members of the Dominican Order. The program envisaged an orderly progression of studies, adapted to the abilities of each Dominican, and one, moreover, which was designed to continue throughout the member's lifetime. One may easily imagine that Thomas Aquinas heavily influenced the development of this program, which he knew would foster in his fellow Dominicans qualities that favored both their acquiring knowledge of sacred truth and their establishing rhythms of evangelical peace. Proper study would enable the Dominicans to fulfill their mission as well-trained athletes in the service of Christ—straight shooters, if you will.

Aquinas artfully deploys a metaphor drawn from archery in one of his biblical commentaries, namely on Job 42:2, "I know that you can do all things, and that no purpose of yours can be hindered." Aquinas affirms that this verse "can refer to the infallibility of divine operation." He then goes on to comment:

> Therefore, just as a skilled archer releases his arrows directly so that he strikes only the target, so when God wishes to release lightning-bolts like some arrows against Leviathan or any other creature, they do not go to any other place but where he releases them, according to Wisdom 5:22, "The emission of lightning-bolts will go directly."[43]

In sum, Aquinas wanted young Dominicans to become like smart archers who make certain that their arrows always hit the mark.

---

43. Thomas Aquinas, *The Literal Exposition on Job: A Scriptural Commentary Concerning Providence*, trans. Anthony Damico (Atlanta: Scholars Press, 1989), 464. The relevant Latin runs: "sicut ergo sagittarius sapiens directe sagittas emittit ita quod non percutit nisi ad signum."

2

Flourishing

The Pope's Man

Because of the place he holds in the history of Catholic thought, as well as his influence on the world's intellectual culture, Thomas Aquinas's life, works, and thought have attracted much scholarly attention. Especially since the publication of a papal encyclical in 1879 that commended the study of Aquinas to Catholics and others, historical research into Aquinas's biography has brought to light a considerable number of details.[1] However, lacunae still exist. For instance, it is not certain to which place Aquinas went immediately after his first Paris regency ended in late June 1259. A general scholarly consensus points toward Italy. Further consensus suggests that wherever he was living, Aquinas began, after Paris, to work on another of his systematic treatises, the *Summa contra Gentiles*. It is a sign of Aquinas's genius that scholars find multiple explanatory theories to account for the inspiration behind the composition of this work. One of the scholars best acquainted with the *Contra Gentiles*, R. A. Gauthier, captures the range of opinions by describing the four-part treatise as one that exhibits the

---

1. For background to Pope Leo XIII's *Aeterni Patris*, see Roger Aubert, "Le Contexte Historique et les Motivations Doctrinales de L'Encyclique 'Aeterni Patris,'" in *Tommaso D'Aquino nel I centenario dell'enciclica "Aeterni Patris,"* ed. Benedetto D'Amore (Rome: Società Internazionale Tommaso D'Aquino, 1981), 15–48.

truths of the Catholic faith set forth as a "wisdom of a universal apostolic bearing."[2] Whatever stands behind Aquinas's composition of this comprehensive account of Christian belief and life, the fact remains that much of the material is presented in a way that makes it useful for undertaking Christian apologetics.

Apologetic arguments usually address those who do not profess the Catholic faith but who nonetheless show a willingness to engage in discussion about it. The practice within the church dates back to the earliest Christian scholars, such as Justin Martyr (d. 165). Those persons who compose an *apologia* search out truths to which natural reason can attain. The great service that the *Summa contra Gentiles* renders its readers is the way that Aquinas examines truths that are open to the inquiry of reason and "shows by many arguments that it was fitting for them to be proposed for belief by supernatural revelation."[3] In other words, he does apologetics and more. Specifically, this *Summa* also expounds on truths such as the Trinity and the incarnation that surpass the whole ability of natural reason to explore and to prove. Aquinas, at the same time, clearly displays that human reason finds nothing repugnant in such mysteries of faith. The *Summa contra Gentiles* bears abundant testimony to Aquinas's keen ability to draw precisely and clearly the distinction between the natural and the supernatural, between faith and reason, between philosophy and theology. In its first three books, this work considers truths that do not exceed the grasp of natural reason. These naturally knowable truths include the existence and attributes of God, the act of creation with its effects, and the dynamics of divine providence. The fourth book of the *Contra Gentiles* investigates divinely revealed truths: the triune God, Jesus Christ, the seven sacraments, and the last things—death, judgment, heaven, and hell. Aquinas thus articulates what human reason can know about God without the grace of divine revelation and how these truths accessible to human reason do not contradict supernatural truths. In other words, Aquinas exhibits the distinction between reason and faith without compromising one's profitable interaction with the other. Although one thinks straightaway of Aquinas's *Summa theologiae*, the

---

2. Jean-Pierre Torrell, *Saint Thomas Aquinas*, vol. 1, *The Person and His Work*, trans. Robert Royal, rev. ed. (Washington, DC: Catholic University of America Press, 2005), 107n49, references the introduction to the Leonine edition of the *Summa contra Gentiles*, edited by Gauthier.
3. The eighteenth-century commentator Bernard de Rubeis (1687–1775) first made this observation. For more information, see Anton C. Pegis, general introduction to Thomas Aquinas, *Summa Contra Gentiles Book One: God*, trans. Anton C. Pegis (Notre Dame: University of Notre Dame Press, 1975), 15–44.

Summa contra Gentiles still provides a valuable summary of his developed teaching.[4]

Martin Grabmann has rightly observed that not every theologian possesses the talent to treat the *duplex ordo cognitionis* (twofold order of knowledge).[5] Indeed, Grabmann's observation, though written in the 1920s, applies to certain intellectual trends of the late twentieth and early twenty-first centuries as much as it does to the supernaturalist movements of the seventeenth and nineteenth centuries to which he adverts.[6] After remarking on Aquinas's ability to sound the harmonies between the orders of faith and reason, philosophy and theology, Grabmann explains what happens when thinkers focus only on faith and theology:

> Philosophical and theological tendencies, on the other hand, which at first glance may seem to bear much more of the supernatural, such as Jansenism, Traditionalism, and Ontologism, have blotted out the distinction between the natural and supernatural. In fact, they so obscured the supernatural that they eventually reduced it to nothing.[7]

In pursuing the harmonies between faith and reason, Aquinas did not innovate. True enough, he and Albert the Great were the first of the medieval thinkers to allow a certain autonomy to faith and science so that each could pursue its proper objectives. At the same time, neither Aquinas nor Albert ever doubted the organic link that binds philosophy and theology. In 1995, the pope, Saint John Paul II, explained the distinctive achievement of authentic Catholic thought with respect to faith and reason. "Faith," writes the pope, "asks that its object be understood with the help of reason; and at the summit of its searching, reason acknowledges that it cannot do without what faith presents."[8] With this citation, the encyclical concludes a section devoted to the contributions of Saint Anselm of Canterbury (d. 1109).

---

4. For a recent examination of the *Summa contra Gentiles*, see Brian Davies, *Thomas Aquinas's* Summa Contra Gentiles*: A Guide and Commentary* (New York: Oxford University Press, 2014).
5. For further information, see Romanus Cessario, "Duplex Ordo Cognitionis," in *Reason and the Reasons of Faith*, ed. Paul J. Griffiths and Reinhard Hütter (New York: T&T Clark, 2005), 327–38.
6. Students of Christian thought often cite twentieth-century figures such as Karl Barth, Henri de Lubac, Hans Urs von Balthasar, and Karl Rahner. See, for example, John Milbank, *The Suspended Middle: Henri de Lubac and the Renewed Split in Modern Catholic Theology*, 2nd ed. (Grand Rapid: Eerdmans, 2014). For a critique of this view, see Steven A. Long, *Natura Pura: On the Recovery of Nature in the Doctrine of Grace* (New York: Fordham University Press, 2010).
7. Martin Grabmann, *The Interior Life of St. Thomas Aquinas: Presented from His Works and the Acts of His Canonization Process*, trans. Nicholas Ashenbrener (Milwaukee, WI: Bruce Publishing, 1951), 24–25.
8. John Paul II, *Fides et Ratio*, no. 42, see also the following sections (nos. 45–48) that treat the "enduring originality of the thought of St. Thomas Aquinas."

Aquinas develops Anselm's intuitions about the faith and reason binomial in a way that continues to govern Catholic theology. One of the best places to discover the originality of his genius may be found in his *Commentary on the* De Trinitate *of Boethius*, questions 1–4. Armand Maurer captures an essential point of these questions that corresponds perfectly to the tenets of Catholic orthodoxy:

> Since both lights come from the same God, philosophy and theology cannot contradict each other. Rather, they are related like the gifts of nature and grace. Grace does not destroy nature but perfects it. Similarly, the light of faith does not do away with the light of reason, but it reveals truths beyond the reach of reason itself. Reason, for its part, can come to the aid of faith in various ways.[9]

The editor of this seminal text of Aquinas's writings enumerates some of these "various ways": establishing the preambles of faith (such as the existence and unity of God), proving many truths about creatures that faith presupposes, and refuting doctrines contrary to the faith by exposing their error or by questioning their conclusiveness. Philosophy can also suggest analogies that help explain the Christian faith. M.-D. Chenu has summarized Aquinas's contribution to the shaping of modern Catholic theology in this way: "Gospel faith brings rational analysis into play in order to clearly explain itself and to take full account of its human significance."[10]

By fall 1261, Thomas Aquinas received a new assignment, a new place from which he would carry on his intellectual service to the church. Because the Dominicans constitute a transnational brotherhood, their members in principle may be assigned anywhere in the world where the Order is established. Ordinarily, however, Dominicans receive assignments within the geographical region or province they entered. Thomas Aquinas belonged to the Roman province of the Order. So it happened that once he completed his term in Paris, Aquinas found himself at home in Orvieto, a picturesque Umbrian hilltop town, which according to the circumstances of the time also sheltered a papal residence. During the roughly eleven hundred years, from 754 to 1870, when the popes enjoyed temporal sovereignty over the central Italian peninsula, they took up residence in various places

---

9. Thomas Aquinas, *Faith, Reason, and Theology: Questions I-IV of His Commentary on the* De Trinitate *of Boethius*, trans. Armand Maurer (Toronto: Pontifical Institute of Mediaeval Studies, 1987), xiv.
10. M.-D. Chenu, *Aquinas and His Role in Theology*, trans. Paul Philibert (Collegeville, MN: Liturgical Press, 2002), 41.

within their realm.[11] Orvieto beautifully afforded one such place. There Aquinas took up the obligations of a distinctively Dominican institution, that of the house lector.

Because of their commitment to study and their conviction that the pursuit of sacred truth affords an authentic path to seek union with God, Dominican governing legislation requires that each priory or convent appoint one member to serve as a house tutor or reader (*lector*). The terminology reflects a time when books were not easily available to everyone, and so in order for many to learn from them, one person was deputed to read (*legere*) the text. Most likely, Aquinas took his appointment as an occasion to help his confreres at Orvieto sort out the theological labyrinths of the book of Job. Christians have always wondered why bad things happen to good people. Aquinas grappled with this question by exposing the literal, not the metaphorical or spiritual, sense of this Old Testament dramatic poem.

The fact that Aquinas held this position in the city where the Roman curia also was residing meant that he was asked to provide useful services to the papacy. He especially rendered these to Pope Urban IV (d. 1264), who was a Frenchman and had studied at Paris, though before Aquinas's arrival there.[12] The pope's business was manifold and various. He requested of Aquinas learned opinions and research on topics that concerned the everyday conduct of the church's business. These assignments included not only issues of social justice, such as discussions of the morality that governs specific aspects of buying and selling, but also what today would be considered ecumenical work, such as doing research that would help the pope heal the split, at once theological and political, that had developed between the Catholic Church and those Christian churches led by the patriarch of Constantinople. Toward this latter end, Aquinas exposed what he found to be the errors of the Eastern theologians, or "the Greeks," as he refers to them, and he supplied arguments to support the prevailing outlooks of Latin theology. His short *Contra errores Graecorum* examines a Latin translation of texts from Greek authorities about which Aquinas expresses reservations concerning these authors' purported use of technical terms like *hypostasis* and *logos*. In *Against the Errors of the Greeks*, Aquinas further examines certain controverted questions such as the procession of the

---

11. The Papal States, over which the pope ruled as a temporal sovereign, included the modern Italian regions of Lazio (which includes Rome), Marche, Umbria, and Romagna, and portions of Emilia. The papal residence moved according to the exigencies of the times.
12. Born Jacques Pantaléon at Troyes in the Champagne region of France, this enterprising pontiff built the Gothic Saint Urban Church on the site of his father's shoemaker shop.

Holy Spirit from the Father and the Son, the primacy of the papacy, the use of unleavened bread during the Mass, and the punishments of purgatory. While Aquinas noted some of the theological imprecisions that he observed in the words and thought of the Greeks, he also attempted to advance a doctrinal reconciliation between the Christian East and West. Progress toward healing the rift, however, did not come immediately; the separation, though mitigated by the removal of the mutual excommunications in 1964, remains even to this day.

The pope's business did not occupy all of Aquinas's time. The *Catena aurea*, in all likelihood, also dates from this period. This golden chain of patristic texts, attached conveniently to the verses of the four Gospels on which they comment, still provides helpful background reading for the Sunday preacher. In the mid-nineteenth century, John Henry Newman and some of his Oxford Movement friends translated this unique Thomist work into English.[13] Aquinas also turned his attention to writings that give plain evidence of Platonist or Neoplatonic influences, such as his *Exposition on the* De divinis nominibus. The treatise *On the Divine Names* comes from the pen of Pseudo-Dionysius, a Christian Neoplatonist of the late fourth or fifth century. As one authority explains the author's purpose, "the burden of *De divinis nominibus* is to show that only a few names can be applied to the Godhead, for God is, in fact, above all conceptions of 'being,' 'goodness,' and the rest."[14] Only God knows fully who he is. However, this transcendence does not imply that God remains anonymous. So Aquinas defends the naming of God, who dwells shrouded in luminous obscurity. Modern Thomist scholarship comes to different conclusions about the presence of Neoplatonism in Aquinas's overall thought.[15] Whatever the definitive evaluation (if one is possible to achieve) may determine about the influence that Platonic themes in general have on Aquinas's systematic works, all scholars agree that the basic philosophical orientation that Thomas Aquinas maintains owes its inspiration to Aristotle. No reasonable person advances the position that Aquinas should be numbered

---

13. Thomas Aquinas, *Catena Aurea: Commentary on the Four Gospels Collected out of the Works of the Fathers*, trans. John Henry Newman (Southampton: Saint Austin Press, 1997). This four-volume edition contains an introduction by Aidan Nichols, OP.
14. James A. Weisheipl, *Friar Thomas D'Aquino: His Life, Thought, and Works* (Washington, DC: Catholic University of America Press, 1983), 175. For further information, see Bernhard Blankenhorn, *The Mystery of Union with God: Dionysian Mysticism in Albert the Great and Thomas Aquinas* (Washington, DC: Catholic University of America Press, 2015).
15. For a noted defense of Platonic and Neoplatonic influence on Aquinas's thought, see Cornelio Fabro, "Platonism, Neo-Platonism and Thomism: Convergencies and Divergencies," *New Scholasticism* 44, no. 1 (1970): 69–100.

among the Platonists. At Orvieto, Aquinas also provided consultations to other prelates. The papal household has always tended to attract visiting clerics, as it does today in Rome. Bishops gather where the pope resides. In addition to serving the needs of the papal curia, Aquinas also generously responded to questions posed by various ecclesiastics and other authorities, which come down to us as letters or "replies" to very concrete inquiries, such as how to confront those Saracens who mock the incarnation. Throughout the latter part of his career, Aquinas took the time to give answers to various questions that he received from all classes of people. Some eighteen of these documents are extant.[16]

Today we tend to think of theologians as tethered to the sterile environments of the professional academies that treat religious studies. Theologians and bishops often find themselves facing confrontation instead of enjoying collaboration. Aquinas would have found our circumstances amusing, if not sad. He, rather, exemplifies what it means to work as an ecclesial theologian.[17] One example of his preference for harmony between the church and the theologian emerges in his readiness to put his hand to liturgical composition. The abovementioned Pope Urban IV asked him to write the liturgical prayers for the official liturgy of a new feast that was to be instituted in honor of the Blessed Sacrament. A eucharistic miracle that occurred close by, at Bolsena, prompted Pope Urban toward this decision. Although Catholic theology does not consider the eucharistic transubstantiation a miracle, inasmuch as the "appearances" remain, the church does recognize miracles that occur around the Eucharist. In this case, a thirteenth-century parish priest, who was wavering in his faith about the Real Presence, discovered blood flowing from the consecrated host, which stained the sacred linens used at Mass. One of them, the corporal, was brought to the pope with the blood marks fresh on it.[18] The Office for the Feast of Corpus Christi reveals a side of Aquinas that may easily escape those interested only in his purely speculative achievements. These texts show Aquinas the poet and even the troubadour. We also discover in the prayers and hymns and other compositions that take up various eucharistic themes concrete expressions of Aquinas's religious devotion.[19] He was a full-hearted Christian believer, as well as

---

16. See Torrell, *Saint Thomas Aquinas*, 1:351–57.
17. For further information, see Congregation for the Doctrine of the Faith, 1990 Instruction, *Donum Veritatis*, On the Ecclesial Vocation of the Theologian.
18. Visitors to the cathedral at Orvieto may still view this blood-stained corporal.
19. See the 1945 essay by Charles de Koninck, "This Is a Hard Saying," in *The Writings of Charles de Koninck*, vol. 2, ed. and trans. Ralph McInerny (Notre Dame: University of Notre Dame Press, 2009),

smart. G. K. Chesterton astutely captures Aquinas's poetic genius when he observes the difficulty of translating into English the *Lauda Sion*, a long Latin poem that serves as the Sequence for Corpus Christi: "How are we to find eight short English words which accurately stand for 'Sumit unus, sumunt mille; quantum isti, tantum ille'?"[20] The question is rhetorical, of course. The short answer appears *sans phrase*: one does not.

Teacher of Grace

Jean-Pierre Torrell meditates on Aquinas's achievements during the roughly five years that followed his teaching at Paris. He draws this conclusion: "The solitude of his priory had nothing of the isolation of an ivory tower."[21] Unfortunately, some modern readers of Aquinas find him interesting solely on account of his argumentation. For scholars of this stripe, his texts provide, as it were, playing fields for their intellectual gymnastics. Or, what is less desirable, they find Aquinas an interesting partner for dialectical engagement with the arguments of other religious thinkers. These ivory-tower approaches admittedly may serve some useful purpose; for example, some bright-eyed young scholar may discover a thinker who delivers more persuasion than what he or she had expected to find in a Catholic theologian. However, to regard Aquinas from the perspective of an analyst or a dialectician thwarts students of Aquinas from learning what he has to teach us about the living God. Because of his capacity to draw people into a living contact with the Truth, the church has repeatedly identified Aquinas as a sure guide for pursuing both theological and philosophical studies. This practical feature of Aquinas's writings explains why, since early on after his death, the church has taken him as its common doctor.[22] Spiffy intellectuals may indeed unearth subtle meanings in his texts, but they can also easily miss the experience of his wisdom.

Pope Urban IV died on 2 October 1264. The next year, though no causal connection may be verified, the Dominicans gave a new assignment to Thomas Aquinas. For his part, Urban's successor, Clement IV

391-98. For a recent study of Aquinas's prayers and hymns, see Paul Murray, *Aquinas at Prayer: The Bible, Mysticism and Poetry* (London: Bloomsbury, 2013).

20. G. K. Chesterton, *Saint Thomas Aquinas* (San Francisco: Ignatius Press, 2002), 128. Chesterton, however, makes a stab at translation and at the same time illustrates his point (in fn. 3): "One receives, a thousand receive; however many they, that much is he."
21. Torrell, *Saint Thomas Aquinas*, 1:141.
22. For further information, see Pierre Mandonnet, "Les titres doctoraux de saint Thomas d'Aquin," *Revue Thomiste* 17, no. 1 (1909): 597-608.

(d. 1268), because of the troubles that still threatened Rome, remained in Umbria. Thomas Aquinas, however, set off for the Eternal City, brigands and all, to establish a study house (*studium*) for young Dominicans. It is generally thought that Aquinas had recognized, even while he was teaching in Paris, the deficiencies that affected clerical training. Although the Catholic priesthood has enjoyed two millennia of existence, our knowledge about how priests have been trained remains sketchy.[23] Catholic priests, of course, require a formation that introduces them to the science of theology. Like any discipline, theology enjoys its own normative structure. One does not discover the unity of the theological disciplines without some principle that serves to unify the various elements (or disciplines) that vie for the theologian's attention. Aquinas identifies the formal interest that unifies the theological disciplines as *revelabilitas*, that is, "all things whatsoever that can be divinely revealed."[24] This precision allows theology, the science of faith, a large field of inquiry, whereas "able-to-be-revealed" (*revelabilitas*) also serves to prevent the reductionist project of regarding all human learning as, in the final analysis, theological.

Theology supplies those who practice it well a vantage point from which to view the world. The proper concern of theologians is God, about whom they can learn from his creatures and also from "what he alone knows about himself and yet discloses for others to share."[25] No higher source of knowledge can be imagined, and so Aquinas finds that the well-trained theologian fits the definition of a wise person. Since they instrumentally communicate divine truth to the world, clerics must discover the sapiential dimensions of theology in order to fulfill their mission adequately. A further complexity results from the fact that while theology first of all concerns itself with speculative matters—such as the nature and existence of God, the mystery of the incarnation, and the instrumentality of the church and its sacraments—the cleric-theologian also must deal with practical matters, mainly in moral theology but also in areas such as sacramental administration and the general field of pastoral care. Aquinas's new assignment posed a significant challenge to his pedagogical abilities. As a result of his

---

23. For one informative but limited study, see Kathleen M. Comerford, "What Did Early Modern Priests Read? The Library of the Seminary of Fiesole, 1646–1721," *Libraries & Culture* 34, no. 3 (1999): 203–21.
24. *Summa theologiae* 1a, q. 1, art. 3. Translation taken from Thomas Aquinas, *Christian Theology*, ed. and trans. Thomas Gilby, vol. 1 (1a. 1) of *Summa Theologiae* (London: Blackfriars, 1964), 13.
25. See *Summa theologiae* 1a, q. 1, art. 6.

having successfully met this challenge, the church received a revised masterwork of Catholic theology.

The *Sentences* of Peter Lombard exhibit an initial attempt to order the various theological materials that the early Middle Ages received, somewhat haphazardly, from the first millennium. *Sentence* commentaries, including what Aquinas himself composed, often came to include many extraneous things, useless arguments, hypothetical questions, and so forth in their treatments of the main areas of theology. Roughly a century of bright and not-so-bright teachers lecturing on the *Sentences* left Lombard's work heavily encrusted with accretions like so many barnacles on a ship's hull. Not everything, therefore, was useful for training clerics and some of it may have even thwarted their comprehension of theology. Aquinas noted this unhappy circumstance, and he, in fact, abandoned an attempt to revise his earlier composition.[26] This left him with a search to find the right textbook. As happens even today, Aquinas came to realize that if he wanted the right textbook for his students, especially for the run-of-the-mill students who remained in provincial study houses instead of going to university cities, he had to write the book himself. This he did.

Exactly when Aquinas began his *Summa theologiae* baffles even the experts on his literary output. What cannot be disputed, however, appears immediately to even the first-time reader of this unfinished master work: the *Summa theologiae* represents the fruit of Aquinas's maturity, both spiritual and intellectual. Aquinas's *Summa* occupies a rock-solid place in the catalog of the world's classical literature. In the twentieth century alone, commentators have set about to explain, to synopsize, to translate, to paraphrase, to outline, and to carry out just about everything else to help readers discover Aquinas's masterpiece.[27] While crib sheets, handbooks, and readers' guides may help the uninitiated student of Aquinas to gain some glimpse of his intellectual world and achievement, nothing surpasses making the effort to read the text itself: *Lege Thomam* (Read Thomas) carries the marching cry for all right thinking Thomists.[28]

---

26. See his general foreword to the *Summa theologiae*. He mentions a swarm of pointless inquiries, ordering according to the requirements of textual commentary, and repetitiousness as reasons for launching a new project.

27. For a good and up-to-date explanation of the work, see Jean-Pierre Torrell, *Aquinas's Summa: Background, Structure, and Reception* (Washington, DC: Catholic University of America Press, 2005). For a well-executed summary, see Michael Dauphinais and Matthew Levering, *Knowing the Love of Christ. An Introduction to the Theology of St. Thomas Aquinas* (Notre Dame: University of Notre Dame Press, 2002).

28. The actual Dominican *Constitutions* (no. 82) give an explanation for the practice: "The best teacher

The material content of the *Summa*, as its title suggests, supplies the reader with a sum of theology. Thomas Gilby (d. 1975) gives as succinct a description of the contents as may be found conveniently in English.

> There are three parts, consisting of questions divided into articles. The first part, *Prima Pars* (1a), is about God and his creatures streaming forth from him. The second part, on the return of intelligent beings to their source, is taken in two movements, the *Prima Secundae* (1a2ae) on human acts, morality, law, and grace, and the lengthy *Secunda Secundae* (2a2ae) which repeats the movement on the virtues in greater detail. Thirdly the *Tertia Pars* (3a) considers Christ "who as man is the way of our striving for God."[29]

The overall comprehensiveness of the *Summa* remains one of its most significant characteristics. Aquinas emphasizes at the beginning of the *Summa* that this work exposes the *sacra doctrina* (holy teaching). The *Summa theologiae* arose out of pedagogical concerns that Aquinas encountered when teaching young students of theology. He wished to communicate to them the truth about God and all things in relation to God. Both the structure and the contents of the *Summa theologiae* reveal God's overarching plan for the salvation of the world that he created. Students learn, then, both from what Aquinas says in the *Summa* as well as how he says it. Because God stands as the ultimate and supreme cause of both creation and redemption, Aquinas considers God as an efficient cause insofar as he creates, conserves, and providentially orders all things. He also places God as the final cause or perfective end of all creatures and of the human creature in particular. One effective means to gain further entrance into what Aquinas accomplishes in his *Summa* comes from the pen of one of his baroque commentators, John of St. Thomas, a text that fortunately exists in a modern English translation.[30] This seventeenth-century theologian summarizes the *Summa*'s structure in this way: "from God considered

---

and model in fulfilling this duty is St. Thomas, whose teaching the Church commends in a unique way and the Order receives as a patrimony which exercises an enriching influence on the intellectual life of the brethren and confers on the Order a special character. Consequently, the brethren should develop a genuine familiarity with his writings and thought, and, according to the needs of the time and with legitimate freedom, they should renew and enrich his teaching with the continually fresh riches of sacred and human wisdom" (*The Book of Constitutions and Ordinations of the Brothers of the Order of Preachers* [Dublin: Dominican Publications, 2012], 63).

29. Thomas Gilby, "Appendix 1: Structure of the *Summa*," in Thomas Aquinas, *Christian Theology*, ed. and trans. Thomas Gilby, vol. 1 (1a. 1) of *Summa Theologiae* (London: Blackfriars, 1964), 44.
30. For a modern edition, see John of St. Thomas, *Introduction to the* Summa Theologiae *of Thomas Aquinas*, trans. Ralph McInerny (South Bend, IN: St. Augustine's Press, 2004); and a review of the book by Romanus Cessario in *Nova et Vetera* 6, no. 3 (2008): 701–3.

in himself and in his being, we pass to God as efficient and redemptive cause, in order to come back to him as the object of happiness after the glorious resurrection. So it is that the golden circle of theology is closed."[31] So, from God as the effective principle of all of reality to God as the finalizing happiness of the human creature to God as the Savior who redeems fallen humanity, the *Summa theologiae* remains theological from beginning to end. What is most important, God always stands at the center of this "golden circle."

Aquinas probably taught the *Summa*, or parts of it, as he was working on its composition. The *Summa* betrays all the signs of a text destined for classroom use and beyond. Unfortunately, he never brought this work to completion. He put away his formal writings on 6 December 1273, less than a year before his death. The *Summa* received its finalization in the form of a supplement his disciples put together by drawing from his early writings. However, it took several centuries after Aquinas's death before the *Summa* replaced the *Sentences* as the major instrument of instruction in theology schools, including those of the Dominican Order.[32]

Altogether, Aquinas spent three years in Rome. He worked on many projects, including the production of commentaries on Aristotle, from whom, one may argue, Aquinas learned how to put an *architecton* at the service of evangelical mission and theological formation. While there can be no dispute that Aquinas worked on philosophical texts and, of course, composed some twelve his own, there exists a difference of opinion among scholars about whether Thomas Aquinas himself should be considered a philosopher. One thing appears certain: Aquinas considered himself at home in the philosophical disciplines, as the distinguished intellectual work of professors such as John F. Wippel amply demonstrates. Further, someone like Professor Wippel remains "convinced that a well worked out metaphysics existed in [Aquinas's] own mind and can be recovered from his various writings."[33] Given the various and diverse efforts at making this recovery, especially the philosophical treaties and textbooks that have presented themselves across many centuries as in conformity with the mind of Aquinas, this conviction seems ungainsayable.[34]

---

31. John of St. Thomas, *Introduction*, 11.
32. The invention of the printing press facilitated the diffusion of the *Summa theologiae*. For a short account of its gradual emergence as a standard textbook, see Torrell, *Aquinas's Summa*, 86–105.
33. See John F. Wippel, *The Metaphysical Thought of Thomas Aquinas: From Finite Being to Uncreated Being* (Washington, DC: Catholic University Press of America, 2000), xvii.
34. For further discussion, see Pasquale Porro, *Thomas Aquinas: A Historical and Philosophical Profile*,

While still in Rome, Aquinas began a project that shows the sensitivity of his character. Because of his importance as a teacher and writer, the Dominicans assigned one of their members to serve Aquinas as secretary and companion (*socius*). One can imagine easily Reginald of Piperno as a loyal, efficient, and careful aide-de-camp for Aquinas, who even in his own day began to draw the attention of crowds. At the same time, there seems no reason to suppose that Reginald's intellectual abilities matched those of his master, whose words he transcribed from dictation. Poor Reginald wrote down so many things that he did not understand that one day, it is reported, he asked his master to write a book that he could understand. The latter obliged with the *Compendium of Theology for Brother Reginald*. Unfortunately, Aquinas was not able to complete the book, which he planned to organize around the three theological virtues of faith, hope, and charity. Events in Paris unexpectedly brought his Italian sojourn to a provisional end. In order to appreciate the seriousness that medieval society attached to events that to twenty-first-century observers may seem like just another set of political complaints from within the educational sphere, it is important to recall the integration of religion and public life that prevailed in the thirteenth-century West, especially in France.

The modern secular mind looks at religion as a compartment of human life that some people attend to more than others. Roughly since the eighteenth-century French revolution, the presumption that there exists a secular world free of all entanglements with God and religion has become a truism within Western democracies. Even citizens who subscribe to a religious creed tend to regard religion as either a private exercise about which the lay political authorities take no notice or a public exercise to which, hopefully, benign political authorities will grant immunity unto the benefit of the civil commonweal. Eighteenth-century revolutions in both France and the United States signal the breaking point with the earlier joint arrangements that governed church and state relations.

Doctor of Truth

To recount the historical twists and turns that mark the evolution in the way that political regimes coexist with religious institutions requires making differentiations of all sorts. Generalizations, there-

---

trans. Joseph G. Trabbic and Roger W. Nutt (Washington, DC: Catholic University Press of America, 2016).

fore, prove very difficult to verify. For example, the French government, which operates under the *laïcité* enshrined in a 1905 law, nonetheless officially sustains some religious institutions. In Mayotte (a French overseas department) in the Comoros Islands, the French prefect appoints the Mufti and the Koranic judges.[35] Twenty-first-century church and state arrangements for a small island in the Indian Ocean, located off the coast of Madagascar, may seem far afield from mid-thirteenth-century Paris. Or, maybe not. Whatever may be the case, the throne and altar arrangements of medieval Christendom created a cultural reality that has disappeared for all practical purposes in the Western democracies. Aquinas's patron, the French king Louis IX, was canonized less than thirty years after he died in northern Africa while on crusade. During the modern period, however, few political leaders have been sainted by the church. Blessed Charles of Austria (d. 1922) stands out as a notable exception, though he died in exile. On the other side of the equation, in only a very few places (e.g., in the Vatican city-state and the principality of Andorra, where the local bishop is the co-prince) do Catholic clerics belong to a distinct and privileged political class.

Although they enjoyed the patronage of sovereigns and princes, the medieval universities of the thirteenth century nonetheless revolutionized education in Christendom. The university ethos did not follow the pattern of the earlier "monastic schools where the teaching personnel inspired only by the love of God, and without haste, or personal ambition, or care for the morrow, prepared the young monk for the reading of the Bible and taking part in religious services."[36] The new universities generated an atmosphere different from that of the countryside monastery. Pope Benedict XVI adverted to this difference when he spoke about the conflicts between the philosopher Abelard and the monk Saint Bernard of Clairvaux. "Now," the pope explained, "whereas St. Bernard, a staunch representative of monastic theology, puts the accent on the first part of the definition [*fides quaerens intellectum*], namely on *fides* faith, Abelard, who was a scholastic, insists on the second part, that is, on the *intellectus*, on understanding through reason."[37] In any event, and speaking in the broadest terms, by the second half of the thirteenth century, this faith–understanding tension erupted in

---

35. See Guy Bedouelle and Jean-Paul Costa, *Les laïcités à la française* (Paris: Presses universitaires de France, 1998), 69–70.
36. M.-D. Chenu, *Toward Understanding Saint Thomas*, trans. A. M. Landry and D. Hughes (Chicago: Henry Regnery Publishing, 1964), 17.
37. Benedict XVI, "General Audience," Saint Peter's Square, Wednesday, 4 November 2009.

Paris amid volatile intellectual exchanges. Into this atmosphere of conflict, the Dominicans brought Thomas Aquinas, now in his midforties, back to Paris, where he arrived in 1268. It appears that the superiors of the Order wanted him there in a hurry since they arranged for Aquinas to travel from Rome to Paris by boat: Civitavecchia to Aigues-Mortes, then up the Rhone to Paris.[38] Once arrived, Aquinas encountered three controversies that agitated the minds of those Parisians who dwelt on the left side of the Seine—the *Quartier Latin*, so called from the practice of using only the Latin language in the classrooms of the medieval schools.

The first controversy concerned how to establish the architectonic structure of Catholic theology. With few exceptions until the High Middle Ages, the majority of recognized Christian theologians drew from Christian authors (or those they assumed to be Christian) when they plied their theological trade. The intuition remains sound. Theology can only proceed properly on the basis of the acceptance of divine revelation, and so the theologian turns first of all to those who, like Saint Augustine, undertook their theological work as believers. One could not rely uncritically on pagan authors to supply the stuff of theological exposition and at the same time preserve the unity of the divine science. This does not mean that the medieval authors of an Augustinian bent were naïve. They knew that Augustine and others had borrowed judiciously from philosophers, even pagan ones like Cicero. However, the boundaries, so to speak, for doing theology were established by Christian authors. The appearance of Latin translations of Aristotle, which did not happen suddenly and all at once but reached a certain high point in the mid-thirteenth century, occasioned the first major challenge to the prevailing and canonized way of doing theology.[39] Conflict—impossible to summarize briefly—arose in Christendom. As his frequent use of patristic texts, especially those of Saint Augustine, illustrate, Aquinas did not reject the views of the ancient Christian writers. At the same time, as his massive and comprehensive *Summa theologiae* reveals, Aquinas recognized that the successful portrayal of Catholic truth required more than edification by beauty, inspiration by light, and moral encouragement by exhortation and example. In short, he opted for a theology that observed the relationship between faith

---

38. Torrell, *Saint Thomas Aquinas*, 1:181–82.
39. For information on recent studies that discuss the arrival Aristotle's texts into the medieval West, see Robert Pasnau, "The Latin Aristotle," in *The Oxford Handbook of Aristotle*, ed. Christopher Shields (Oxford: Oxford University Press, 2012), 665–89.

and reason that he had explicated in detail during his first stint in Paris when he commented on Boethius's *De Trinitate*.

The church grants Aquinas "a quite special place" in the development of a harmony between the knowledge of faith and the knowledge of philosophy "because of the dialogue which he undertook with the Arab and Jewish thought of his time."[40] Subjacent to this dialogue stands the towering figure of Aristotle, citations from whom in the *Summa* alone require eighteen nine-by-five-inch book pages to index.[41] However the Parisian theologians of 1268 were a long way from accepting the argument that the establishment of any harmony between pagan Aristotle and Jesus Christ would prove desirable. "What indeed," as Tertullian famously remarked, "has Athens to do with Jerusalem?"[42] Aquinas, one may aver, would have answered the question along positive lines. Chesterton surely thinks so. He, with a certain trustworthy intuition, summarizes what one may reasonably conclude about Aquinas and Aristotle: "Whether or no he baptized Aristotle, he was truly the godfather of Aristotle; he was his sponsor; he swore that the old Greek would do no harm, and the whole world trusted his word."[43] Certain contemporary theologians fume over a remark like this. The plain and inescapable fact, however, remains: Chesterton is right.

The second controversy that Aquinas faced arose from an improper appropriation of philosophical tenets into the world of Christian life and practice. Philosophical explorations about natural things like animals, vegetables, and minerals usually occasion no difficulty for Catholic teaching. Philosophical musings about man, however, easily brush up against sound Christian convictions that either flow from tenets of faith or are tied closely to revealed truth.[44] In the thirteenth century, one such nefarious musing erupted in what may be termed Averroist monopsychism—the belief that all human creatures share a single separate intellect—named after the Spanish polymath Ibn Rushd, known to the Latin West as Averroes (d. 1198). Aquinas refers to him simply as "The Commentator."[45] He meant, of course, the commentator on Aristotle's treatises, which supply a good example of a

---

40. See *Fides et ratio*, no. 43.
41. T. C. O'Brien, *General Index*, vol. 61 of *Summa Theologiae* (London: Blackfriars, 1981), 20–37.
42. Tertullian, *De praescriptione haereticorum*, chap. 7.
43. Chesterton, *Saint Thomas Aquinas*, 108.
44. For a remarkably erudite account of how Aquinas treats the degrees of natural life, see John F. Boyle, *Master Thomas Aquinas and the Fullness of Life* (South Bend, IN: St. Augustine's Press, 2014), 16–40.
45. For erudite commentary on Aquinas's use of Averroes, see Rémi Brague, *Eccentric Culture: A Theory of Western Civilization*, trans. Samuel Lester (South Bend, IN: St. Augustine's Press, 2009), 108–9.

whole complex of literature and learning that came to be known as Aristotelianism.[46]

An emblematic figure for the radical Aristotelians of thirteenth-century Paris (sometimes known as Latin Averroists) appears in the person of Siger of Brabant, who taught in the arts, not in theology. Again, this controversy does not succumb to short explanations. One author puts the neuralgic issue that radical or heterodox Aristotelians exposed as follows: they "tend to be willing to embrace doubt about personal immorality as a possible consequence of a strict hylomorphic position."[47] The run up to this unhappy circumstance proceeds something like this: as long as the human soul informs a material body, the soul cannot carry out the properly immaterial (or spiritual) acts of the mind required for human knowing. These immaterial acts, then, are explained by appeal to a common agent intellect located in a higher realm than where the human race dwells. Thus, these confused Aristotelians advanced a practical monopsychism, which in turn makes a Christian view of personal responsibility and destiny difficult to uphold to the extent that individuals would remain passive instruments of a single, higher mind.

Aquinas's interaction with these "radical" thinkers exhibits his characteristic sangfroid. He could have retreated to traditional anthropological models, which stress the complete spiritual substance of the soul but leave open questions of how the soul and body are united. Instead, Aquinas distinguishes. He explains that an immaterial soul can use a material body as an instrument for knowledge, even unto attaining a natural knowledge of God. Aquinas in his *De unitate intellectu* (*On the Unity of the Intellect*) minced no words when he argued against Siger's positions. Aquinas did more than win an argument. Some hold on evidence that as a result of Aquinas's strong defense of the truth about the human psyche, Siger recanted his erroneous views about a separate agent intellect located above the dwelling place of any human person.[48]

The third controversy that faced Aquinas after his boat trip up the Rhone River emerged as a recrudescence of a conflict in which he had already engaged, namely the defense of the mendicant religious life. The discussions, disputations, and writings from this second round of

---

46. For further discussion, see Edward Grant, *God and Reason in the Middle Ages* (Cambridge: Cambridge University Press, 2001), 88–89.
47. Joseph W. Koterski, *An Introduction to Medieval Philosophy: Basic Concepts* (West Sussex: Wiley-Blackwell, 2009), 196.
48. See Grabmann, *Interior Life*, 62–63.

anti-mendicant quarrels required Aquinas to respond to certain underhanded practices that the opponents of the Dominicans and Franciscans employed to deter young men from joining their ranks. Aquinas took the matter seriously, as the closing words of his *Contra retrahentes* (*Against Those Restraining*) illustrate: "If any man desires to contradict my words, let him not do so by chattering before boys but let him write and publish his writings, so that intelligent persons may judge what is true, and may be able to confute what is false by the authority of the Truth."[49]

During the second period of his teaching at Paris, Aquinas continued to carry on his multiform intellectual pursuits. Specifically, the regent master produced writings on the books of the Bible, which, again, tally up throughout his lifetime to eleven works based on sacred books from both Testaments. In addition, he conducted more disputations and specialized disputations (quodlibetals); these allowed the Paris university community to ask of a master whatever question, philosophical or theological, that may have left them with disquiet of soul or just curious. Aristotelian commentaries and answers to requests for expert opinions complete the list of works that Aquinas composed. In short, he continued the work of a Paris regent master. One should not be surprised to learn that according to the best evidence, Thomas Aquinas enjoyed the services of several secretaries to whom he would give dictation. Sometimes, it is said, Aquinas kept busy as many as four secretaries at a time.[50]

---

49. *Contra doctrinam retrahentium a religione*, in *An Apology for the Religious Orders*, trans. John Procter (London: Sands, 1902).
50. See Torrell, *Thomas Aquinas*, 1:241–42.

3

Denouement

Christ Only

When Aquinas left Paris in spring of 1272, he had less than two years of life on earth ahead of him. According to custom, Aquinas installed his successor in one of the Dominican chairs at Paris, a friar named Romanus of Rome, who would die before the end of his own regency. Perhaps under the influence of another crowned head, Charles of Anjou, younger brother of Saint Louis, Aquinas was charged to inaugurate a *studium* (study house) in a Naples now under Angevin rule. In any case, the royal treasury would pay him an ounce of gold a month for teaching there. Change of venue did not effect a change in Aquinas's adherence to a form of life or his following of a pattern of work. He returned to the Dominicans in Naples, where he had started his religious life. There Aquinas took up the rhythms that throughout the course of his Dominican life afforded him the time to accomplish as much as he did. More learned composition flowed from his pen and, instrumentally, those of his secretaries. These include biblical commentaries and the continuation of work on his *Summa theologiae*. One also may observe that his residing in Naples again put Thomas Aquinas geographically close to his family. On several occasions, he profited from their hospitality and support.

Close reading of the available historical documents does not sustain the view that Aquinas confined his activities exclusively to prayer, study, and teaching. He is also known to have dealt with downright practical matters, such as serving as the executor of a relative's will, which required his undertaking delicate negotiations with both family members and the royal court, since the deceased relative was a nobleman. In addition, Aquinas continued to participate actively in the political governance of the Dominican Order. His standing as a master of sacred theology enfranchised him to attend both provincial and international meetings. Scholars have identified nineteen texts of sermons that Aquinas preached; without a doubt, these represent only a portion of the preaching that he delivered in various pastoral settings. Some sermons are linked to places, such as Milan, where Aquinas is known only to have passed through. One may conclude safely that he was a sought-after preacher. Aquinas also attended to the sweet side of life. Once he invoked the intercession of Saint Agnes, an early virgin martyr, in order to obtain the healing of his dedicated companion and hardworking scribe, Reginald of Piperno. In gratitude for his friend's recovery from a bout of ill health, Aquinas initiated a practice that may surprise the casual reader of only his speculative writings. On the feast day of the saint, 21 January, Aquinas arranged that the Dominicans would serve a special dessert or sweet to those who shared a common refectory or dining room with him. Earlier in his career, he hosted the customary banquet after his installation as a master of theology with monies that he had reserved for this purpose. Aquinas also wept, especially when certain liturgical pieces were sung during the choral celebration of the Liturgy of the Hours. Because he wrote so much, the temptation exists to think that we know all about the man. As with any saint, we will discover only in heaven the complete dimensions of Aquinas's personality and his genius.

In early December of 1273, Aquinas stopped his literary production. One may still visit the medieval chapel preserved within the later construction of the fourteenth-century Dominican church in Naples where Aquinas encountered Christ in a profoundly spiritual way.[1] *Non nisi Te*, replied Aquinas in response to Christ's offer of a reward for his well-accomplished theological writings. "Nothing but you, O Lord" has become a motto for properly educated Thomists, who are not at all surprised to discover this documented episode at the end of Aquinas's life. In his *Summa theologiae*, Aquinas said straight out, "Christ above all oth-

---

1. In the Basilica of San Domenico Maggiore, Piazza S. Domenico Maggiore, Naples.

ers is wise and a friend."² For whom else had Aquinas been working so hard? The medieval chronicles and other credible documentation lead one to believe that Aquinas's last months on earth were marked by certain health problems. None though, so it appears, were serious enough to keep him from starting out on a journey toward Lyons, France. There, the fourteenth ecumenical council, the Second Council of Lyons (1272-1274), was meeting to discuss, among other items, the schism that divided Latin and orthodox Christianity. Aquinas brought with him his *Contra errores Graecorum*. On the way north, illness overtook him, and after resting briefly at a relative's home (where he asked for fresh herrings to eat), Aquinas was transferred on a litter to the Cistercian Abbey of Fossanova located just off the ancient Via Appia. There he lingered for almost a month before his death on 7 March 1274. The Cistercian monks, who had maintained this monastery since the early twelfth century, took advantage of Aquinas's presence to request his help with interpreting the Song of Songs. As mentioned above, unfortunately no manuscript of these sick-bed conferences has been found.

Miracle Worker

According to general practice at the time, Aquinas was to be buried in the place where he died. His funeral liturgy at Fossanova drew Dominicans as well as dignitaries both ecclesiastical and civil. At the end of the obsequies, his body was buried close to the main altar of an abbey church built in the Cistercian Gothic style of architecture.³ Each of these twelfth-century movements, Gothic architecture and the Cistercian Order, find their origin within the confines of *la belle France*. This circumstance of divine providence befits the impact that Thomas Aquinas made on the various intellectual movements whose developments almost always centered on thinkers who worked around the University of Paris.

On Wednesday, 2 May 1274, authorities of the University of Paris, together "with all the masters at present teaching in the faculty of

---

2. *Summa theologiae* 1a-2ae, q. 108, a. 4, sed contra: "Sed Christus maxime est sapiens et amicus." Translation taken from Thomas Aquinas, *The Gospel of Grace*, ed. and trans. Cornelius Ernst, vol. 30 (1a2ae. 106-14) of *Summa Theologiae* (London: Blackfriars, 1972), 61.
3. The relics of Aquinas have undergone various translations since 1274. They presently reside in the Church of the Jacobins in Toulouse, where they were sent originally for safekeeping by order of the pope in 1369. At the time of the French Revolution, the relics, in 1791, were put, again for safekeeping, in the Basilica of Saint-Sernin. On 7 March 1974, the seventh centenary of his death, they were returned to the remarkably refurbished Église des Jacobins, which remains a monument to the achievements of both the Dominicans and French architects.

arts," wrote to the Dominicans to express their grief at the news of Aquinas's death. They further argued that Paris alone merited to serve as the place of burial for him "whose youth was nourished, fostered, and educated here at Paris, which then received from him in return the inexpressible benefit of his teaching."[4] In addition to this touching tribute to Aquinas's intellectual achievement, the authorities also requested certain of his works—all of a philosophical nature—that they understood were in his possession when he died. It has been justly remarked that no mention of the theology faculty appears in this letter. Rather, philosophers and other "artists" exhibited solicitude for the philosophical works of Aquinas.[5] No record of a response from the Dominicans to this request exists.

As mentioned above, the church recognizes Thomas Aquinas as a saint. John XXII, one of the popes who kept his residence in Avignon, made the proclamation on 18 July 1323. After his election at Lyons, this pope lived at the Dominican priory in Avignon, which may explain the exuberance attributed to his eulogizing of Aquinas: "He has wrought as many miracles as he has written articles."[6] The math is off, but the church did recognize, according to the criteria in vigor, ninety-six miracles attributed to the intercession of Thomas Aquinas. The first of which occurred in the Cistercian abbey church of Fossanova when a blind monk received his vision back while praying at Aquinas's bier.[7] Devotion to Saint Thomas Aquinas remains ardent in the church. Pope John XXII designated 7 March, the day Aquinas died, or the day of his birth into heavenly glory (*dies natalis*), as his liturgical feast day, and so it remained until after the reforms of the Second Vatican Council when the feast was transferred to 28 January, the day in 1369 when the relics of Aquinas reached the Church of the Jacobins in Toulouse.[8]

---

4. For an English translation of this document, see Kenelm Foster, ed., *The Life of Saint Thomas Aquinas, Biographical Documents* (Baltimore: Helicon Press, 1959), 153–57.
5. For further information, see James A. Weisheipl, *Friar Thomas D'Aquino: His Life, Thought and Works* (Washington, DC: Catholic University of America Press, 1983), 332–33. See also Foster, *Life of Saint Thomas*, 154n7.
6. Jean-Pierre Torrell, *Saint Thomas Aquinas*, vol. 1, *The Person and His Work*, trans. Robert Royal, rev. ed. (Washington, DC: Catholic University of America Press, 2005), 321: "et quod tot fecerat miracula quod scripserat articulos."
7. Ibid., 297. For more hagiographical reports, see John Placid Conway, *Saint Thomas Aquinas of the Order of Preachers (1225-1274): A Biographical Study of the Angelic Doctor* (London: Longmans, Green, 1911).
8. For further information about the transfer of relics, see MSM editorial services, *The Jacobins Convent in Toulouse*, trans. Barbara Jachowicz-Davoust (Vic-en-Bigorre, France: MSM, 2009), 22–23.

Light of the Church

One miracle did not happen. Radical Aristotelianism continued to gain ground among the Parisian masters of arts, even though the better part of them had lamented Aquinas's passing.[9] The theologians, for their part, became more suspicious than before about the use of pagan philosophers, notably Aristotle and Averroes, as tools for elaborating Christian theology. Even during Aquinas's lifetime, in 1270, the bishop of Paris, Stephen Tempier, condemned thirteen explicit radical Aristotelian (Averroist) theses. Little seems to have come of this condemnation, however. Concern among the theologians of Paris continued to mount with respect to philosophical errors that were, in their view, inimical to the Catholic faith. This concern came to the attention of the pope, John XXI, who himself was the author of a philosophical textbook (*Summulae logicales*). He asked for an accounting from Bishop Tempier, and this request resulted in the compilation of 219 propositions that, according to judgments apparently gathered from diverse theology professors, merited condemnation. Among other effects, this action, which was officially promulgated on 7 March 1277—three years to the day after Aquinas's death—meant that the condemned theses were, under threat of serious penalty, excluded from classroom instruction. Within the same month, a shorter list of condemned theses was published in Oxford by the Dominican archbishop of Canterbury, Robert Kilwardby.

The Oxford list brought to the fore a dispute that would haunt Aquinas's legacy for a half century after his death. Weisheipl summarizes the matter succinctly: "For Thomas Aquinas the simultaneous presence of many substantial forms in a single composite is a metaphysical impossibility, since the very first actualization of first matter constitutes the substance and the essence of creatures."[10] For the traditional theologians, both Dominicans and Franciscans, including John Pecham, Kilwardby's successor, this fairly abstruse piece of philosophy affected how the theologian would be able to explain that the body of Christ, both when dead on the cross and when in the tomb, remains divine. To safeguard the divinity of Christ's soulless body, the standard theological opinion before Aquinas postulated the presence of a corporeal form to give the body divine standing. Aquinas, on the other hand,

---

9. Weisheipl (*Friar Thomas D'Aquino*, 333–40) can be counted on to give an ample explanation of these controversies, which had at their heart philosophical issues.
10. Ibid., 337.

argued for the permanence of the incarnation and the hypostatic relationship of the dead body of Christ to his divine Person. In other words, he developed an explanation that did not require the metaphysically clumsy, to say the least, to appeal to the presence of more than one substantial form in a single reality. It is not unreasonable to inquire why a rather technical question of this kind would have generated such strong feelings. The answer lies not in philosophical preference but in a certain theological thoroughgoingness. Medieval theologians felt obliged to ensure the divinity of the dead Christ in order to account for the eucharistic real presence in the event that the apostles had celebrated Mass during the *Triduum Sacrum*.[11]

The condemnations of 1277 have been the subject of considerable research. While in the first half century after his death, Aquinas moved toward canonization, those, including some unfortunate Dominicans, who pursued the new Aristotelian learning in any form whatsoever fell under suspicion. Truth to tell, while Thomas Aquinas appointed no successor, he immediately found defenders. The Thomist legacy needed them. Around 1279—that is, shortly after the condemnations at Paris and Oxford—the Franciscan William de la Mare took on himself the job of correcting what he took to be suspicious passages in Aquinas's writings. He then published a list of these corrections that Franciscans especially and others should observe when reading Aquinas. William called his work a *Correctorium*. The Dominicans dubbed it a *Corruptorium*, a book of corruptions of Aquinas, and no less than five young Dominican scholars produced replies to what they obviously considered an affront to their confrere's intellectual integrity.[12] Although the Franciscans earlier joined Dominicans as allies against the secular masters who wanted to exclude them both from the university, this happy coalition fell apart over the question of how churchmen should develop theology. The theological bearings taken by Dominicans and Franciscans continued to diverge. Dante obviously had hoped to recall the original complementarity of the two mendicant orders when he describes Thomas Aquinas and the Franciscan Bonaventure of Bagnoregio in sweet exchanges with one another: "The bright courtesy of brother Thomas, and his well-judged speech, stirred me [Bonaventure] to praise of so great a knight [Saint Dominic], and stirred this company with me."[13] As events developed, Aquinas's views were vin-

---

11. See *Summa theologiae* 3a, q. 81, art. 4.
12. See Torrell, *Thomas Aquinas*, 1:305–8.
13. Dante, *Paradiso*, Canto 12:106–45.

dicated. Shortly after Aquinas's canonization, the Paris condemnation of 1277 was lifted, specifically, from those propositions "insofar as they touch or seem to touch the doctrine of the aforesaid Blessed Thomas."[14] Oxford bypassed this formality as anticlimactic.

---

14. Weisheipl, *Friar Thomas D'Aquino*, 349.

PART II

The Thomists, or "The Heritage of Truth"

4

Uneven Beginnings

Condemnation and "Correction"

Monumental aptly characterizes the academic achievement of Thomas Aquinas. Even early on, popes recognized this quality of his person and work. "Just as Saint Thomas shines among all the doctors by the beauty of his style and of his thought, likewise this church in Toulouse surpasses in beauty all the other churches of the Friars Preachers. I chose it for Saint Thomas and I wish that his body find its place there."[1] Thus declaimed Pope Urban V (d. 1370), himself a Frenchman who had studied in the Rose City twained by the River Garonne. This sixth and penultimate of the Avignon popes resolved longstanding disputes over the final resting place of Saint Thomas's earthly remains. The choice of Toulouse also honored Saint Dominic, who, with his first followers, took possession in 1216 of the city's Saint-Romain chapel.[2]

---

1. "Discours du Cardinal Jean Guyot" in "VIIe centenarie de saint Thomas d'Aquin et retauration de l'égilse des Jacobins," ed. Bureau de l'Association du Centenaire de saint Thomas d'Aquin (Toulouse, 1976), 25; for further information, see É. Delaruelle, "La translation des reliques de saint Thomas d'Aquin à Toulouse (1369) et la politique universitaire d'Urbain V," *Bulletin de littérature ecclésiastique* 56, no. 3 (1955): 129–46.
2. For further information, see M.-H. Vicaire, *Histoire de Saint Dominique*, vol. 1, *Un Homme Évangélique* (Paris: Les Éditions du Cerf, 1982), 341. The author emphasizes that this choice associated the Dominicans with the urban development and educational movements of the period. Also see M.-H. Vicaire, *Histoire de Saint Dominique*, vol. 2, *Au Coeur de l'Église* (Paris: Les Éditions du Cerf, 1982), 57–58.

Except for an unhappy interlude after the French Revolution when they were moved for safekeeping to another church in Toulouse, the relics of Saint Thomas still reside in the church where Pope Urban V—who, it should be noted, had begun his clerical life as a Benedictine monk—ordered them transferred in 1369. Admittedly, Aquinas's academic legacy provides historians with a more difficult challenge than that posed by his earthly remains. Nonetheless, his intellectual monument, or, as Josef Pieper calls it, "the heritage of truth," that the interpreters of Aquinas, since his death in 1274, have constructed finds a fittingly symbolic representation in the Dominican church at Toulouse.[3] This imposing Gothic edifice, consecrated in 1385, goes under the name of the Église des Jacobins, a sobriquet used in France for the Order of Friars Preachers.

The heightened prominence that philosophy gained in the university settings of Europe from the start of the thirteenth century generated anxiety among certain theologians. In a word, the quarreling over substantial forms betrayed a sharp difference of opinion among Christian thinkers about how generously they should allow philosophy to throw light by analogy on the contents of faith.[4] Aquinas's views were well-known. "If we resolve the problems posed by faith," he once said, "exclusively by means of authority, we will of course possess the truth—but in empty heads!"[5] The debates that emerged revealed divided views on the broad methodological question of how philosophy and authority figure in to the development of Christian theology. Skittishness about just how much philosophy should play a role in theological discussions created a deep skepticism toward Aquinas's characteristic "boldness" about human reason.[6]

The condemnation of certain theses both at Paris and Oxford in 1277, three years after the death of Aquinas in Italy, created a highly charged atmosphere in the intellectual centers of Europe. Although Aquinas's name appeared in neither list of banned opinions, those persons who had not yet grown congenial to his innovations in the sacred sciences made the condemnations an occasion for advancing their unreconstructed views. This group mainly included local bishops

---

3. Josef Pieper, *The Silence of Saint Thomas*, trans. John Murray and Daniel O'Connor (Chicago: Henry Regnery Publishing, 1965), 104.
4. See Aquinas, *De Trinitate* q. 2, art. 3, resp.
5. Thomas Aquinas, *Quodlibetal Question* IV, art. 6, as cited in M.-D. Chenu, *Aquinas and His Role in Theology*, trans. Paul Philibert (Collegeville, MN: Liturgical Press, 2002), 26.
6. The word comes from Pope John Paul II, *Fides et ratio*, no. 48: "The *parrhesia* of faith must be matched by the boldness of reason."

and university professors, though even the reigning pope, John XXI, imposed disciplinary measures to support Bishop Tempier's condemnations at Paris. This pope died shortly thereafter, on 20 May 1277; still, his mention of both philosophers and theologians who "dogmatize errors" seemed to implicate Aquinas.[7] The next pope, Nicholas III (d. 1280), proceeded to appoint a onetime opponent of Aquinas, John Pecham, a Franciscan theologian, to the archbishopric of Canterbury. Pecham continued his advocacy of the doctrine of plurality of substantial forms and insisted that Catholic orthodoxy depends on it. There followed, in the words of one scholar, "an active period of controversy in which the Franciscan prelate enjoyed a temporary advantage."[8]

In order to put this controversy in perspective, one must remember the theological teaching that Aquinas's opponents feared would be imperiled by their agreeing with those who upheld the Aristotelian position that no composite substance can have more than one substantial form. Bishops and some theologians worried about how to explain the divinity of the dead body of Christ. As events developed, Pecham's conundrum led to his taking a less than generous view of Aquinas's philosophical agility. One expert on the subject explains:

> For Pecham this was not simply a philosophical issue, but one that touched the roots of Christian faith. If man has only one substantial form, he argued, then the living body of Christ on the cross cannot be the "same body" of Christ in the tomb. Pecham argued that there must be a "corporeal form" that is identical for both bodies. He and others even argued that if Mass had been celebrated while Christ was dead, it would not be true to say, "This is my Body," or "This is my Blood."[9]

Archbishop Pecham was persuaded that his opinion enjoyed the authority of Saint Augustine and that any other approach to the problem of the identity of Christ's dead body would lead to heresy. Modern scholarship has determined otherwise about the antiquity of this philosophical analogy. The so-called doctrine of plurality of forms actually came into currency in the twelfth century.[10] Aquinas, as we have seen, advanced a different theory to explain the divine status of

---

7. James A. Weisheipl, *Friar Thomas D'Aquino: His Life, Thought, and Works* (Washington, DC: Catholic University of America Press, 1983), 335.
8. Frederick J. Roensch, *Early Thomistic School* (Dubuque, IA: Priory Press, 1964), 14–15.
9. Weisheipl, *Friar Thomas D'Aquino*, 289.
10. See Daniel A. Callus, "The Origins of the Problem of the Unicity of Form," in *The Dignity of Science: Studies in the Philosophy of Science Presented to William Humbert Kane, O.P.*, ed. James A. Weisheipl (Washington, DC: Thomist Press, 1961), 121–49.

Christ's dead body. His approach, however, did not entail heresy and, at the same time, avoided the metaphysical clumsiness that arises from postulating two substantial forms in one concrete, substantial being.[11] Aquinas was an innovator, however. In the late 1270s, partisans on each side of the question drew their battle lines around the philosophical question of the plurality of substantial forms.

Other confusions arose about how the new Aristotelian learning would affect the practice of Christian theology. Sixteen of the theses prohibited at Paris and three of those at Oxford reflected ideas found, though considerably qualified, in Aquinas's writings.[12] Still, his critics tried to tar Aquinas with the same brush as the radical Aristotelians. Sometime between 1277 and 1279, the Franciscan theologian William de la Mare, who had succeeded John Pecham in the Franciscan chair at Paris, drew up a list of 118 topics from the works of Aquinas that required, in his view, emendation in light of the official condemnations that had been issued by the ecclesiastical authorities. The work, the *Correctorium fratris Thomae*, both gave its name to a controversy and earned for its author the—in hindsight—dubious title of the first systematic Neo-Augustinian. Because the debates were carried on mainly between members of the Dominican and Franciscan Orders, the *Correctorium* quarrels, as mentioned above, set each of these newly established mendicant orders at odds with the other.

As the motto of their Order, *Veritas* (Truth), might suggest, the Dominican scholars at Oxford, where the controversy initially flared up, did not remain supine in the face of opposition. The Yorkshire man William Hothum (d. 1298), who though a Dominican died archbishop of Dublin, followed the teaching of Aquinas and, what is more important, defended it. Hothum, whose career was spent largely attending to the diplomatic affairs of the English king, Edward I (d. 1307), came to the defense of those who tried to uphold Aquinas's positions. That a man of Hothum's standing took up the cause of one substantial form suggests that, even shortly after his death, an *esprit de corps* centered on Aquinas's teaching had begun to develop among at least some of his Dominican confreres, including the superiors. Hothum served twice as provincial. The exact occasion that gave rise to Hothum's defense of Thomist views involved another English Dominican, Richard Knapwell (d. ca. 1288), who produced one of the "Correctoria Corruptorii" writings. His composition comes down to us with the title "Quare," or "Why

---

11. See *Summa theologiae* 3a, q. 76, art. 1, ad 1.
12. For a list of theses, see Weisheipl, *Friar Thomas D'Aquino*, 336–37.

do you disparage words of truth?" It was a question addressed to the Franciscan William de la Mare.

As already mentioned, the Dominicans were not willing to let William de la Mare get away with impunity. On the contrary, they accused the Franciscan of distorting Aquinas's thought. Indeed, William's Dominican interlocutors gibingly referred to his work as a "corruption" (*corruptorium*) instead of a correction (*correctorium*). Knapwell was the first to step into the ring. The plight of this staunch defender of the unicity of substantial form earned him rebuke and condemnation, including a temporary excommunication at London, which the pope eventually lifted. The papal reprieve, however, did not spell papal endorsement of Knapwell's Thomist views. Instead, Pope Nicholas IV (d. 1292), the first pope drawn from the ranks of the Franciscans, imposed on the frazzled Knapwell a perpetual silence about the controversial theses. Knapwell returned to the Dominicans at Bologna, where he died, some say, having become unhinged as a result of the treatment he had received. Those teachers who raised questions such as, "Whether faith about the essence of human nature united to the Word requires us to posit plurality of forms," were playing for high stakes. The uninitiated contemporary student of theology may be excused for thinking the brouhaha, well, odd. On the other hand, Catholic theology would have taken a different turn were the Augustinian theologians to have prevailed in their intransigence.[13]

The "Correctoria" literature continued to appear. At least five of these texts survive. A second comes from the pen of another English Dominican, Robert Orford, about whom little biographical information is available other than that he preached a sermon at Oxford on the second Sunday of Lent in 1293. He produced his "Sciendum" or "It Should be Known that Thomas . . . ," which also took issue with each of the 118 corrections that William de la Mare thought necessary to make Aquinas safe for Augustinian theology. The third of the genre deals with only sixty of William's complaints. The *Correctorium* "Circa," or "About question XII, art., 2_0," comes from the pen of the Parisian scholar Jean Quidort (d. 1306). Like the other Dominicans engaged in the "Correctoria" controversy, Quidort wrote on a wide variety of subjects. His straightforward defense of Aquinas's work against false charges places this Frenchman within the burgeoning group of Dominicans one may describe, even if somewhat anachronistically, as

---

13. For an account of the Augustinian teaching and objections to Aquinas, see Roensch, *Early Thomistic School*, 170–99.

Thomists. Given the high-profile politics of the times, Quidort himself fell under the suspicion of local ecclesiastical authorities. Like Knapwell, he also appealed to the pope. Quidort, however, died awaiting a final judgment on his appeal; nothing, however, survives about the state of his mental health. We owe the fourth *Correctorium*, "Quaestione," to the English Dominican William Macclesfield (d. 1303), who, unlike his confreres, may have died a cardinal of the Roman Church.[14] The title indicates that the author begins his riposte by treating *Summa theologiae*, question 12, article 2, "Does the mind see the essence of God by means of any created likeness."[15] Macclesfield defended Aquinas's view of the spirituality of the separated substances and of the human soul and refuted the fondly held Franciscan opinion that both angels and human souls are composed of form and "spiritual matter."[16] In order to explain the created status of both angels and the human soul, he "frequently emphasized that the composition of matter and form is not to be made coextensive with that of potency and act."[17] A fifth reply to William de la Mare comes from the Italian Dominican Rambert dei Primadizzi (d. 1308), who was working in Paris. His "Apologeticum veritatis contra Corruptorium" stands incomplete, but his intention remains clear: to mount an apologetic of truth against the "Corruptorium" of William de la Mare.

What significance may be drawn from this episode in medieval intellectual history? That five young Dominicans, none of whom were university masters at the time, launched a strong defense of Aquinas's thought gives one moment for pause. They and their unknown collaborators and sympathizers formed the nucleus of a new school of thought. The *Correctoria* literature does not represent intramural academic wrangling among junior scholars who had nothing better to do with their time. The *Correctoria* controversy rather reveals, among those who took up the cause of Aquinas's teaching, the birth of a tradition that one rightly calls Thomist. These young scholars did not lack some institutional support. The Dominican Order supported the teaching of their "venerable father Friar Thomas d'Aquino." As early as 1278,

---

14. Pope Benedict XI created Macclesfield, who may have already been dead in England, cardinal titular of Santa Sabina (the Dominican general headquarters in Rome) on 18 December 1303.
15. For a succinct explanation of how the separated soul sees God, see Thomas Aquinas, *Knowing and Naming God*, ed. and trans. Herbert McCabe, vol. 3 (1a. 12–13) of *Summa Theologiae* (London: Blackfriars, 1964), xix–xx.
16. That the human soul is composed of a form and "spiritual matter similar to that of the angels" derives from Saint Bonaventure's own teaching. See Armand A. Maurer, *Medieval Philosophy: A History of Philosophy* (New York: Random House, 1962), 143–44.
17. Roensch, *Early Thomistic School*, 221; for an overview of Macclesfield's arguments, see ibid., 218–23.

a year after the issuance of the condemnations, the supreme governing body of the Dominican Order, the general chapter, forbade any show of disrespect for Aquinas's writings. Subsequent chapters in 1279, 1286, and 1309 issued statements that increasingly made Thomas Aquinas a recognized authority within the Order.[18] Further, several of those who went public with their defense of Aquinas also later received ecclesiastical preferments. At least some of the Dominican participants in the *Correctorium* battles belonged to the political mainstream. Although a few of these young Dominicans fell under temporary censures, they did not make up an eccentric band of dissident outsiders.

Disagreements over Papal Teaching Authority

Did the earliest debates that developed around the teaching of Thomas Aquinas raise only philosophical topics? Further, did they treat subjects that today, it may be thought, would prove interesting mainly to intellectual historians? It seems not. First, as mentioned above, the philosophical topics that generated conflict point to changing outlooks about the nature of theology, the role of authority in Christian thought, and how human knowledge reaches God. Furthermore, philosophical opinions were not the only *points chauds* that ignited controversy. Early followers of Aquinas also took up questions that arose from theological disagreements. For example, a few years after the death of Aquinas, the Franciscan Peter John Olivi (d. 1298) developed a polemic on religious poverty that opened up a new front in the conflicts between Franciscans and Dominicans. Because the new mendicant orders contributed so much to the renewal of the church in the thirteenth and fourteenth centuries, their controversies quickly became the concern of the popes. When certain Franciscans made unsustainable claims about the requirements that the evangelical counsel of poverty imposes on those who profess it, aspersions were cast on those mendicants who, for example, practiced individual poverty but allowed corporate ownership of the necessities. The Dominicans responded. Much as the battle over the unicity of form was linked to theological concerns about the status of the dead body of Christ, so disputes over the practice of poverty generated commentary on another theological question, namely, the nature of papal teaching authority. As one expert puts it, "Hidden in a doctrine of poverty that had at first glance seemed so harmlessly pious was an explosive question of faith and authority."[19] As

---

18. For a brief account, see Weisheipl, *Friar Thomas D'Aquino*, 242–43.

we have seen, for his part, Aquinas was clearly a pope's man. His earliest commentators were bent on upholding his devotion to the papacy.

In addition to his documented service to the Holy See, the best witness to Aquinas's own regard for the authority of the Petrine office comes from testimony given at the First Canonization Enquiry held from 21 July to 18 September 1319 at the archbishop's palace in Naples. Bartholomew of Capua, a high ranking court official, testified that upon his death bed Aquinas spoke these words about his intellectual output: "If I have said anything amiss, I leave it all to the correction of the Roman Church."[20] Besides, it is impossible to imagine that a Dominican who had spent considerable time close to the papal curia and, on occasion, in personal service to the Roman Pontiffs did not understand what role the pope plays in making determinations about Catholic teaching. Further, unlike certain canonists of his day, Aquinas never mentions the possibility that a pope could fall into heresy. Rather, when he discusses the formulation of creeds that express the fundamental truths of Catholic faith, Aquinas ascribes to the Roman Pontiff an authoritative role that, in turn, requires adherence by all believers with a "steadfast faith" (*inconcussa fide*). Were one to object that Aquinas's views on papal infallibility do not seem as robust as the common teaching of the Catholic Church after the declaration of the First Vatican Council (1869–1870), *Dei Filius* (1870), the best answer to this allegation would point out that the questions and the categories of the nineteenth century were not his own. "Nevertheless," according to one observer, "the answer [Aquinas] did give considerably influenced later discussions" about the nature of papal pronouncements.[21]

When it came to settling questions of Franciscan poverty, even popes found their teaching authority strained by political wrangling. On the one hand, a pope such as Nicholas III (d. 1280), who appointed John Pecham to Canterbury, aimed to settle the question of absolute poverty by declaring meritorious the Franciscans' observance of a rule that enjoined a complete lack of corporate possessions. This settlement, published in Nicholas's bull, *Exiit qui seminat* (14 August 1279), favored the opinion of Franciscan Peter John Olivi about what Christ did or did not own. Olivi had argued that Christ and his apostles owned nothing. At the same time, Olivi inveighed against Aquinas's view that

---

19. Ulrich Horst, *The Dominicans and the Pope: Papal Teaching Authority in the Medieval and Early Modern Thomist Tradition*, trans. James D. Mixson (Notre Dame: University of Notre Dame Press, 2006), 28.
20. For the complete text and further information, see Kenelm Foster, ed., *The Life of Saint Thomas Aquinas: Biographical Documents* (Baltimore: Helicon Press, 1959), 110.
21. Horst, *Dominicans and the Pope*, 20.

since Judas was the bursar of the apostles, one may not claim that Christ lived in "highest poverty," that is, without any ownership. Aquinas, indeed, taught this fairly obvious fact of the New Testament. In his commentary on John 12:6, he says straightforwardly:

> Two things can be noted here. First, that Christ lived on alms as a poor person: "As for me, I am poor and needy" (Ps 39:18). Secondly, it is not opposed to perfection to keep alms in a money box. Thus what we read in Matthew (6:34), "Do not be anxious about tomorrow," does not forbid one from saving for tomorrow, since our Lord did this very thing, and he is the supreme model of perfection.[22]

The bull of Pope Nicholas, which may not have reflected the pope's settled views on the matter of religious poverty, moved the Dominicans to muse on the nature of papal teaching authority. In other words, they again stood up for Aquinas's teaching as well as their own settled observances, though without adopting a rebellious attitude toward the pope.

During the first thirty years of the fourteenth century, writers within the Thomist tradition took up the question of papal authority. Their treatises represent at least a Dominican school position, one moreover that remained actionable during the discussions that preceded the solemn declaration on papal infallibility in 1870.[23] At the same time, these fourteenth-century authors developed their views on the matter to coincide with Aquinas's clear position on the legitimacy of a reasonable kind of poverty that the vowed religious should embrace. They again displayed the Thomist *esprit de corps*. Some forty years after *Exiit qui seminat*, another pope modified the church's approach to absolute poverty. Indeed, John XXII, the same pope who canonized Aquinas—and did so while the question of radical poverty was being actively debated around the papal court at Avignon—settled

---

22. Thomas Aquinas, *Commentary on the Gospel of John: Chapters 6-12*, trans. Fabian R. Larcher and James A. Weisheipl (Washington, DC: Catholic University of America Press, 2010), 266, no. 1604. See also Thomas Aquinas, *Commentary on the Gospel of John: Chapters 13-21*, trans. Fabian R. Larcher and James A. Weisheipl (Washington, DC: Catholic University of America Press, 2010), 33–34, no. 1821: "Some might also wonder why our Lord had a purse, since he told his disciples, 'Carry no purse, no bag, no sandals' (Lk 10:4). . . . We could say that when he told them to take nothing on their way, he was referring to individual preachers and apostles, who should carry nothing when they went to preach. But it did not refer to the entire group which would need something for themselves and for the poor."

23. See Horst, *Dominicans and the Pope*, 3: "The intervention in the First Vatican Council of the Dominican cardinal Filippo Maria Guidi, who criticized a papal infallibility without certain conditions, was the last attempt to orient the discussion of the late medieval and early modern theologians of the cardinal's order."

the poverty debate in favor of the Dominican position. His bull, *Cum inter nonnullus* (1323), pronounced the thesis that Christ and his apostles did not own anything "erroneous and heretical."[24] To the charismatically charged adherents of the absolute poverty thesis, this exercise of papal teaching authority seemed to reverse the earlier approval given by Pope Nicholas III, even though this pontiff clearly envisaged that another pope might dispose of the question other than he had. In any case, discussion ensued about whether a pope can change important determinations made by his predecessors.

Let three examples suffice to show the modes of theological temper regnant among nascent Thomist writers. The eminent John of Naples represents a typically successful Dominican of the fourteenth century. He began his professional teaching career at the Naples Dominican priory in 1300. Then he went on to receive his credentials at Paris before returning to Naples as the regent of studies for the Dominicans. This distinguished master of theology was the only one of his rank to testify before the canonization enquiry of 1319 about Aquinas's sanctity. John later advanced the cause for canonization at the papal court in Avignon. Eventually, he delivered there one of the several panegyrics that celebrated Aquinas's sainthood. Despite the ample literary indications of John's professional activity, neither the date of his birth nor death is known. Estimates place his death around 1350. What remains incontestable? John of Naples's extant works indicate that he aspired to carry on a Thomist tradition. Well before Aquinas's canonization, John defended at Paris in 1316 the thesis that the doctrine of Aquinas "could be taught at Paris with respect to all its conclusions."[25] At the same time, because this defender of Aquinas's views may have missed some elements of his teaching, Étienne Gilson puts scare quotes around "Thomist" when said of John.[26] This qualification indicates that the Thomist tradition, even though supple among its earliest exponents, undergoes a purification as it develops. The resources that enable this process of purification—for example, access to printed editions of Aquinas's works—were not available in the early fourteenth century. Whatever erraticisms appear in his works, John of Naples found himself charged with examining one of the first and most notorious anti-Thomist Dominicans, the French arriviste Durandus of Saint-Pourçain

---

24. Ibid., 29.
25. Foster, *Life of Saint Thomas Aquinas*, 4.
26. Étienne Gilson, *History of Christian Philosophy in the Middle Ages* (New York: Random House, 1955), 748.

(d. 1334). On the question of papal authority, the Neapolitan affirmed after 1324 a continuity between what was stipulated by the bulls of Nicholas III and John XXII. In sum, John of Naples confronted radical Franciscan poverty and disallowed claims that it enjoys the blessing of the church.

Another Dominican who held several important positions in the Order illustrates Thomist thought from France. Hervaeus Natalis (de Nédélec) died at Narbonne shortly after Aquinas's canonization in 1323. Early in his academic career, however, Natalis defended, perhaps for the first time, the corporate instruction that Aquinas bequeathed to succeeding generations; Natalis called his work, "Defensio doctrinae fratris Thomae."[27] Natalis, who enjoys the title *Doctor Rarus*, authored at least forty treatises on diverse subjects. His several administrative offices brought him into contact with significant controversies of the day, including supervising the close scrutiny to which Dominicans subjected their own nominalist renegade, Durandus of Saint-Pourçain. After Pope Nicholas's bull was issued, Hervaeus Natalis composed a *De potestate papae* (1317–1318) that set forth a representative Dominican view on papal powers. To allow for the odd, off-handed papal remark about corporate possession, Natalis distinguishes between the pope as a "public" and as a "private" person. He further aired the view that certain conditions, which he failed to specify, needed to be fulfilled in order for a pope to deliver a binding determination. This kind of thinking arose during a time when the Holy See supplied a sort of court of last instance to arbitrate the conflicting opinions that an unbridled exercise of dialectical theology easily generates. No one person could keep up with their emergences here and there. One may interpret Natalis's Dominican position as an effort to establish papal authority as an ultimate check on skepticism. Posthumously, his work played a significant role in the controversy that followed the appeal that the Franciscan partisans of absolute poverty made to the Holy Roman emperor Louis IV—called the Bavarian—against the determination of Pope John XXII. The *Appeal of Sachsenhausen* (1324) argued that what a pope defines in faith and morals "cannot be called into doubt by any successor."[28] Were this appeal successful, which it was not, the propo-

---

27. For further information on "The Defense of the Doctrine of Brother Thomas," see *Thomistenlexikon*, ed. David Berger and Jörgen Vijgen (Bonn: Verlag Nova et Vetera, 2006), 266–73. This important lexicon provides biographical and recent bibliographical references for many Thomists.
28. Horst, *Dominicans and the Pope*, 29.

nents of absolute poverty would have received their papal approbation back. They also would have left the church in a serious bind.

The fourteenth century ushers in a period of uncertain times that left serious thinkers with a daunting challenge. They were obliged to find ways to answer "the question about the foundation and the certainty of theological statements and thus of our knowledge of salvation."[29] Dominicans never shied away from the challenge. A third carrier of the Dominican view on papal authority appears in the person of Peter of Palude (d. 1342), who fulfilled the many public roles that fell to Dominicans during this period. He was a scholar, a diplomat, and a curial official who joined both John of Naples and Hervaeus Natalis on the commission set up to judge the nominalist theses of Durandus. If allowance is made for the purification of thought that the development of the Thomist tradition requires, Peter ranks among those who privileged the views of Aquinas, even though he may appear less well-informed about some of them. In any case, irenic Peter argued for continuity between the two papal bulls that *prima facie* would seem to contradict each other on the subject of what ownership the authentic exercise of poverty allows. To support his claim, he cites the counsel that Pope John XXII received from advisors as grounds for ascribing more authority to his bull than that of Nicholas III. While the various prominent Dominicans who took up the question of papal teaching authority exhibit modest differences in their approach to a question that, among thinkers of less nuance, can veer toward privileging the popes' advisors or even a church council over a pope himself, they show unanimity in their desire to sustain their Dominican and Thomist convictions about how the mendicant religious should observe their vow of poverty.

A Fallow Time

The sampling of early Thomist controversies leaves unmentioned the other people and places where the achievement of Aquinas found propagators and interpreters. In addition to Dominicans in England, France, and Italy, *A Catalogue of Thomists*, a standard reference for identifying Thomist authors, lists a few thirteenth-century Dominicans in Germany, Spain, and Scandinavia who wrote Thomist works.[30] Aquinas

---

29. Ulrich G. Leinsle, *Introduction to Scholastic Theology*, trans. Michael J. Miller (Washington, DC: Catholic University of America Press, 2010), 182.
30. Leonard A. Kennedy, *A Catalogue of Thomists, 1270–1900* (Houston: Center for Thomistic Studies, 1987), 35–38.

even found a follower among the secular clergy in the person of Peter of Auvergne (d. 1304), whose large philosophical corpus shows him to have been an active participant in the philosophical discussions that continued after 1274. As any standard history of the Middle Ages confirms, other intellectual movements continued or took root during the decades that followed the death of Aquinas. Still, throughout the fourteenth century, Thomist authors among the Dominicans appear, in addition to the countries already cited, in Armenia, Bohemia, and Poland. Other authors, including those drawn from Benedictine monks and Augustinian hermits, appear in Europe, Byzantium, and elsewhere. In fact, some of the significant representatives of the Thomist tradition are found outside of Europe. Maximus Planudes (d. 1310), Gregory Akindynos (d. 1348), Demetrios Kydones (d. 1398), and Prochoros Kydones (d. ca. 1369; Demetrios's monk brother) produced Greek translations of some of Aquinas's works, including the *Summa theologiae*. Demetrios's attraction to Aquinas led to his entering into full communion with the Holy See, whereas his younger brother died a monk, though one excommunicated by the Greek patriarch for his polemical reaction to Palamism. This admonition appears perfectly understandable given Prochoros's attraction to Aquinas's preference for the "boldness of reason."[31]

While Dominicans were upholding Aquinas's position in a variety of circumstances during the decades that followed his death, another intellectual movement was taking shape among the mendicants. The Franciscan scholars John Duns Scotus (d. 1308) and William of Ockham (d. 1347) initiated a style of thinking (represented differently in each) that attracted followers especially from among their fellow Franciscans.[32] Scotus appears frequently as a dialogue partner with Thomists. Thomas Sutton (d. ca. 1315), who belongs to the early English Thomist school at Oxford, may fall among the first interpreters of Aquinas to take issue with Scotus's views. On the other hand, Ockham fell under suspicion at the Avignon papacy because he took the side of the Franciscans who espoused absolute poverty. Pope John XXII excommunicated Ockham shortly after the Franciscan philosopher sought refuge at the court of Emperor Louis of Bavaria. Some have seen in this flight

---

31. Further discussion of these and other similar Byzantine figures appears in Marcus Plested, *Orthodox Readings of Aquinas* (Oxford: Oxford University Press, 2012).
32. For a brief survey, including accounts of Scotus and Ockham, see Kenan B. Osborne, ed., *The History of Franciscan Theology* (St. Bonaventure, NY: Franciscan Institute, 1994).

a symbolic moment that marks the end of a period in Western civilization.

> When William of Ockham fled from the Minorite cloister to the German imperial court . . . he was traversing the same path but in a reverse direction, as was traversed at the beginning of the epoch by Cassiodorus when he abandoned his political office at the court of the Gothic king and retired to the cloister.[33]

Cassiodorus (d. ca. 585), an associate of Boethius, the "first scholastic," symbolically represents the new birth of learning that the Christian monasteries made possible in the West.[34] He established himself at Vivarium, the monastery-school that included a cenobitic monastery and a retreat for those who desired a more solitary life. Ockham's disobedience marks the start of a recrudescent tension between civil and religious authorities.

In October 1347, the Black Death arrived in Europe. The uncontrolled spread of the disease wreaked havoc over the next seven years. At the request of the French king Philip VI, forty-nine medical masters from the Parisian university, in a document known as the Paris *Consilium*, set forth explanations about the cause of this plague drawn from medieval and ancient authorities. They also wondered whether the causes would ever be known.[35] The effects of this pestilence, however, were painfully evident. Estimates vary but tens of millions died, probably about one-third of the European population. It is difficult to estimate the social upheaval that the Black Death wreaked, especially in Italy and France. There were not even enough priests to administer the sacraments, as one contemporary witness reports.[36] War also affected life in France and England. The Hundred Years' War, a series of battles between France and England, continued until the mid-fifteenth century. The French king Philip VI engaged the English king Edward III at Crecy in northern France on 26 August 1346. The English longbows, as Shakespeare's *Henry V* celebrates, struck a victory. When Philip VI died in 1350, his viscera would find a burial place, according to the custom

---

33. Josef Pieper, *Scholasticism: Personalities and Problems of Medieval Philosophy*, trans. Richard Winston and Clara Winston (New York: McGraw-Hill, 1964), 155.
34. See Romanus Cessario, "Boethius, Christ, and the New Order," in *New Directions in Boethian Studies*, ed. Noel Harold Kaylor Jr. and Philip Edward Phillips, Studies in Medieval Culture 45 (Kalamazoo, MI: Medieval Institute Publications, 2007), 157–68.
35. For further discussion, see Faye Marie Getz, "Black Death and the Silver Lining: Meaning, Continuity, and Revolutionary Change in Histories of Medieval Plague," *Journal of the History of Biology* 24 (1991), 270.
36. Ibid., 269.

of the times, at the Dominican convent of Saint Jacques in Paris. Bellicose strife between England and France, which eventually, in 1431, would ensnare Joan of Arc, continued for almost a hundred years.

5

Identity and Defense

Thomist Coalescence

Certain early interpreters of Aquinas exhibited a more comprehensive grasp of his thought than did others. One of these thoroughgoing Thomist figures appears in the person of William Peter Godin (d. 1336). A native of the Gascony region of France, Godin illustrates the kind of "man for all seasons" style that Dominicans before him like William Hothum and John of Naples embodied. In other words, Godin served both the Dominican Order and the church in a variety of official capacities. Notably, he executed well various ecclesiastical-political missions confided to him by several popes, with the result that he gained standing in the hierarchy. This Dominican Thomist died the cardinal bishop of Sabina, one of Rome's seven suburbicarian dioceses that holds special importance within the College of Cardinals, of which Godin was appointed dean in 1323. As he stipulated in his last testament, however, Godin eschewed interment in either Rome or papal Avignon and instead chose the Dominican church at Toulouse for his burial place. The general consensus holds that Godin's writings show him to remain faithful without demur to Aquinas's teachings. Godin's fidelity appears concretely in his *Lectura Thomasina*, produced during the 1290s, and several philosophical treatises that deal with topics such as the unicity of the intellect, the eternity of the world, and the principle of individuation. During his Paris regency, around 1305, Godin disputed face-to-face with the Franciscan John Duns Scotus on the principle of individuation, that is, how to distinguish one thing from other things within the same class or species. Thomists and Scotists still solve differently the puzzle of individuation—a fact of life that, while obvious to sense observation, remains nonetheless easier to observe than to explain.

Other followers of Aquinas engaged serious disputes outside of the university classroom. For instance, one of the biographers of Aquinas, Bernard Gui (d. 1331), defended Catholic orthodoxy against heretics. In fact, Gui remains widely known to the general public—thanks especially to Umberto Eco's novel *The Name of the Rose*—for his work with the Inquisition. Gui's literary output not only includes handbooks for judging heresies and other deviations, such as sorcery and divination, but also chronicles—that is, composes historical narratives—about Catholic institutions, including the papacy. This erudite Dominican, who died a bishop in France, was also a cultivated Thomist, who in 1323 authored a *Vita Sancti Thomae Aquinatis* that still serves as a main source for information about Saint Thomas's life.[1] Other Dominicans of the period have left biographical materials about Aquinas. They include William of Tocco (d. 1323), author of a *Vita Sancti Thomae*, as well as Bartholomew of Lucca (d. 1327), who mentions Aquinas in his *Historia ecclesiastica nova*. Another Italian layman, Bartholomew of Capua (d. 1328), produced a list of Aquinas's works, *Catalogus operum Sancti Thomae*.[2] There exist other literary witnesses to the fact that, especially after his canonization, Aquinas's life and works became the object of special attention and care by Dominicans and others.

The Black Death did not leave Dominican houses unscathed; a third if not more of the Order's membership succumbed to the plague. During a period of great confusion, some interpreters of Aquinas appeared in unexpected guises. Saint Catherine of Siena (d. 1380), who was born the same year that the Black Death struck Europe, was a Dominican lay tertiary who, among other noteworthy accomplishments, proved instrumental in leading Pope Gregory XI (d. 1378) from Avignon back to Rome. As they approach the Vatican, visitors today encounter a monument to Catherine, whom Pope Pius IX declared a co-patroness of Rome. Later, in 1970, another pope aptly described the kind of inter-

---

1. For further discussion, see Kenelm Foster, ed., *The Life of Saint Thomas Aquinas, Biographical Documents* (Baltimore: Helicon Press, 1959), 1–23.
2. Jean-Pierre Torrell (*Saint Thomas Aquinas*, vol. 1, *The Person and His Work*, trans. Robert Royal, rev. ed. [Washington, DC: Catholic University of America Press, 2005], 270), says that "this list has no right to the title 'official catalogue,' which it was given" by an earlier historian of Aquinas.

preter that Catherine served for Aquinas: "It is true that her writings reflect the theology of the Angelic Doctor in a surprising degree, yet that theology appears there bare of any scientific clothing."[3] That a woman doctor of the church such as Catherine continues to attract modern spiritual authors—more than one thousand publications were devoted to her during the first half of the twentieth century—as well as her influence on subsequent spiritual masters, such as Teresa of Ávila (d. 1582) and Francis de Sales (d. 1622), supports the view that Thomist categories possess a certain timelessness. For that contribution alone, Catherine of Siena merits a notable place among the Thomists.

Catherine of Siena's "surprising" reflection of Aquinas's teaching distinguishes this Dominican woman mystic from the Order's Rhineland spiritual authors like Henry Suso (d. 1366) and John Tauler (d. 1361), who came under the influence of John Eckhart (d. 1328) and his radically negative or apophatic theology. Anti-intellectual religious sentiment has long taken note of Tauler. For example, a nineteenth-century American Quaker poet puts these words on the German Dominican's lips: "My prayer is answered. God hath sent the man / Long sought, to teach me, by his simple trust, / Wisdom the weary schoolmen never knew."[4] The "man" is Eckhart. This exercise of poetic license should not obscure the fact that both Suso and Tauler maintained solidly Catholic allegiances, though the latter, at least, considered Eckhart's views on spirituality incomparably more sublime than those of Aquinas.[5] For her part, Catherine of Siena embraced Aquinas's knowledge mysticism. Catherine's ordering of knowledge and love, as her principal work, *The Dialogue*, displays beyond doubt, remains solidly Thomist:

> By the light set in the mind's eye Thomas [Aquinas] saw me [eternal Truth] and there gained the light of great learning. . . . For love follows upon understanding. The more they know, the more they love, and the more they love, the more they know.[6]

In 1999, Pope John Paul II declared Catherine of Siena and two other women saints—Bridget of Sweden (d. 1373) and Edith Stein (d. 1942),

---

3. Homily of the Holy Father Paul VI at St. Peter's Basilica, 4 October 1970.
4. John Greenleaf Whittier, "Tauler," in *The Complete Poetical Works of John Greenleaf Whittier* (Boston: Houghton Mifflin, 1904), 53, lines 59–62.
5. See Johannes Tauler, "Sermon 29 [Feast of the Holy Trinity II]," in *Johannes Tauler: Sermons*, trans. Maria Shrady (New York: Paulist Press, 1985), 105.
6. Catherine of Siena, *The Dialogue*, trans. Susan Noffke (New York: Paulist Press, 1980), 155–57.

a Jewish convert known as Teresa Benedicta of the Cross who found inspiration in Saint Thomas—co-patronesses of Europe.

History reveals, as already noted, that not only Dominicans but others as well interpret and follow Aquinas. His appeal reaches beyond Catholic denominational loyalties. The Carmelite scholar Guido Terreni (d. 1342) ranks among the early infallibilists who supported, along with the Dominicans, the cause of Pope John XXII when he withdrew papal confirmation from the proponents of absolute poverty. The fourteenth-century infallibilists were those thinkers who preferred to reconcile apparently disparate claims made by the popes rather than impute error to one or another of them. By the end of the fourteenth century, however, questions of papal infallibility gave way to more serious issues about where the ultimate authority in the church resides. The Great Schism (1378–1417), which followed the Avignon papacy—sometimes called the "Babylonian Captivity" since the popes resided for about forty years (1309–1377) outside of Rome—produced three rival claimants to papal office. Thomists such as John de Torquemada (d. 1468), from Valladolid, turned their attention to practical issues of church polity and organization. Torquemada's *Summa de Ecclesia* became, before the sixteenth-century Council of Trent, the most important manual for resolving questions about the functioning of the church. Torquemada knew Aquinas's views on papal authority thoroughly, as the Spaniard's *Flores Sententiarum beati Thomae de auctoritate summi pontificis*, a florilegium of seventy-three opinions drawn from Aquinas on the subject of papal authority, demonstrates.[7] Torquemada contributed mightily to the success of Pope Eugene IV (d. 1447) in his struggle to fend off various conciliarist efforts aimed at introducing democracy into the government of the church. Both pope and theologian found support in texts of Aquinas, such as the tenth question of his disputed question, *De Potentia*.[8] This high-ranking Spanish prelate used

---

7. See Ulrich Horst, *The Dominicans and the Pope: Papal Teaching Authority in the Medieval and Early Modern Thomist Tradition*, trans. James D. Mixson (Notre Dame: University of Notre Dame Press, 2006), 37n76.

8. See Thomas Aquinas, *On the Power of God*, trans. English Dominican Fathers (Westminster, MD: Newman Press, 1952), q. 10, art. 4, ad 13: "Now just as a subsequent Council has the power to interpret the Creed of a previous Council, and to insert an explanation of what that Creed contains . . . even so the Roman Pontiff can do this of his own authority, since by his authority alone can a council be convoked, and by him are its decisions confirmed, and since from the Council appeals can be made to him: all of which is clear from the Acts of the Council of Chalcedon. Nor does such an explanation require the assembling of an ecumenical council, since sometimes this is impossible on account of war: thus we read of the sixth Council that the Emperor Constantine found that he was prevented by the imminence of war from summoning all the bishops together: and yet those who met decided certain doubtful points of faith in accordance with the mind of Pope Agatho."

his position to ensure that the newly invented printing press found its way to Rome and that Thomist books began to appear in print.

Elsewhere, theological controversies between Thomists and the followers (mainly Franciscans) of Scotus continued to take on new directions. John of Montesono (d. 1412), an Aragonese Dominican from Valencia who began his Paris teaching in 1387, kindled a debate that would set Franciscans and Thomists at odds with each other for about the next 450 years. During his inception as a master at the University of Paris, John took issue with the doctrine of the Immaculate Conception of the Blessed Virgin Mary as expounded by Scotus. The latter brought into currency the claim that Mary was preserved from the contagion of original sin. Following Aquinas, John of Montesono defended the traditional doctrine, namely that Mary was sanctified in the womb of her mother.[9] Mary's sanctifying grace, argued Aquinas, was powerful, even rendering the sparks of sin ineffective. After Christ's birth, moreover, Mary shared in her Son's immunity even from these incipient inclinations toward sin.[10] At the same time, Aquinas thought that Mary was cleansed of original sin, not prevented from contracting it. This controversy over the mode of Mary's sanctification remained an active one until the middle of the nineteenth century when Pope Pius IX proclaimed the dogma of the Immaculate Conception.[11] Neutral observers agree that the papal bull, "Ineffabilis Deus" (1854), took account of the Thomist perspective on Mary's prerogative, which insisted on linking her holiness to Christ's foreseen merits. Scotus had envisioned other reasons for explaining this privilege.

Flashpoints in the development of the Thomist school enjoy the advantage of illustrating the versatility of issues and events that the interpreters of Aquinas, even within a century after his death, exerted themselves to address. At the same time, as the extant manuscripts show, everyday instruction in classrooms also continued. The Thomist works produced during the fourteenth century, mainly by Dominicans, indicate that a good number of interpreters of Aquinas spent their time conducting the normal courses of instruction required for the formation of the clergy. For example, an early-fourteenth-century exposition on the gospels appears in Conrad Ruffi's *Compendium expositionis S. Thomae in evangelia*. In addition, texts have survived of both disputed

---

9. See *Summa theologiae* 3a, q. 27, art. 2, ad 2.
10. See *Summa theologiae* 3a, q. 27, art. 3.
11. For further discussion, see Romanus Cessario, "Mary in the Thomist Commentatorial Tradition," in *Sapienza e libertà: Studi in onore del prof. Lluís Clavell*, ed. Miguel Pérez de Laborda (Rome: EDUSC, 2012), 81–88.

and quodlibetal ("whatever") questions authored by Dominican professors who were teaching in the several European countries where regional or international centers of study were established. Thomists also composed liturgical pieces honoring Aquinas and commemorating the translation of his relics to Toulouse. In addition to those already mentioned, other historical treatises documenting the life and the canonization of Aquinas appeared. From the start, Thomists imitated both their master's learning and piety. And for the classroom where new generations of young clerics were being trained, Thomists produced their own commentaries on the *Sentences* and compendia of Aquinas's writings on Lombard's masterwork. One notable late-fourteenth-century textbook, the *Thomasina, Seu compendium S. Thomae in I-III Sententiarum*, by Thomasinus of Ferrara (fl. 1390), was quoted by Edward Bouverie Pusey in his *First Letter* to John Henry Newman on the Blessed Virgin Mary and her Immaculate Conception.[12]

Thomists and Their First Interlocutors

The intellectual achievement of John Duns Scotus maintained its own momentum after his death at Cologne in 1308. Scotism coalesces around the start of the fifteenth century, when its adherents include an assortment of professors, prelates, and princes. The several branches of the Franciscan Order contributed to the sustaining of interest in the *Doctor Subtilis*, as Scotus was nicknamed. The Conventual Franciscans or *Cordeliers* especially kept Scotus's thought alive at their school in Padua. During the sixteenth and seventeenth centuries, universities accorded a special chair or professorship dedicated to the exposition and defense of the Scotist theses. These university positions, in addition to the one at Padua, were located in Paris, Rome, Coimbra, Salamanca, Alcalá, and Pavia. A fifteenth-century Scotist, Angelo Carletti (d. 1495), composed a celebrated handbook of moral theology, the *Summa Angelica*, which enjoyed widespread usage among Catholic priests who heard the confessions of the faithful. It is said that this work appeared with the *Summa theologiae* on the list of books Martin Luther would have liked to have seen burnt in 1520 at Wittenberg.[13]

---

12. E. B. Pusey, *First letter to the Very Rev. J. H. Newman, D.D.: In explanation chiefly in regard to the reverential love due to the ever-blessed Theotokos, and the doctrine of her immaculate conception; with an analysis of Cardinal de Turrecremata's work on the immaculate conception* (Oxford: James Parker, 1869), 440.
13. For a Lutheran perspective, see John Warwick Montgomery, "Luther and Libraries," *The Library Quarterly* 32, no. 2 (1962): 133–47. For a Catholic account, see Hartmann Grisar, *Luther*, vol. 2, trans. E. M. Lamond, ed. Luigi Cappadelta (London: Kegan Paul, Trench, Trübner, 1913), 51.

If true, Luther may be praised for his inclusiveness. A French Franciscan, Bartélemy Durand (d. 1720), who flourished during the late seventeenth century, was a notable exponent of the Scotist tradition. His *Clypeus Scotisticae theologiae contra novos eius impugnatores* provides, as the title suggests, Scotist armor for those who wish to defend the Franciscan doctor against his then recent critics.[14] Not a few of the latter would have been Dominicans. Although Scotism maintained a discreet presence through the eighteenth century, its influence worldwide remained circumscribed. Nonetheless, the positions of John Duns Scotus continue to provide points of engagement for Thomist interpreters, although today these exchanges mainly interest historians of philosophy.

During the second half of the fourteenth century, a broadly influential school of thought emerged that sustained the philosophical emphases and predilections of William of Ockham (d. 1347). The nominalist outlook in philosophy, whose advent well antedates the fourteenth-century debates in logic and metaphysics, arises out of earlier medieval discussions concerning the status of universals.[15] However, the nominalist movement in which Ockham stands out as the originating figure changed the intellectual landscape of the late medieval period in a way that the earlier skirmishes did not. Someone like Roscelin of Compiègne (d. ca. 1125), a representative figure of early medieval nominalism, enjoyed no intellectual posterity even though Peter Abelard was one of his pupils.[16] Post-Ockham nominalism, on the other hand, appeared poised to eclipse the metaphysical achievement of Thomas Aquinas. "In the second half of the fourteenth century," observes one historian of the period, "Thomism and Scotism were already called the 'old way' of philosophizing and theologizing in contrast to the 'modern way' (*via moderna*) of William of Ockham and his followers."[17] The shift of paradigms that takes place in the mid-fourteenth century, as Josef Pieper has observed, finds symbolic representation in the flight of William of Ockham to the protective custody

---

14. Early printed editions appeared at Marseille (1685, 1700) and Venice (1709, 1746).
15. Standard encyclopedia accounts of the school of thought distinguish two kinds of nominalism, "one that maintains that there are no universals and one that maintains that there are no abstract objects." For further information, one may consult, among other sources, Gonzalo Rodriguez-Pereyra, "Nominalism in Metaphysics," *The Stanford Encyclopedia of Philosophy*, Summer 2015 Edition, last revised 1 April 2015, http://tinyurl.com/zubc394.
16. See Étienne Gilson, *History of Christian Philosophy in the Middle Ages* (New York: Random House, 1955), 153–55.
17. Armand A. Maurer, *Medieval Philosophy: A History of Philosophy* (New York: Random House, 1962), 243.

of Louis of Bavaria, where Ockham—his attention turned exclusively to political writings—remained for the rest of his life. The "modern way" introduces and probably contributes to the formation of "dangerous processes" that would bring about future troubles for the church and certainly for the interpreters of Aquinas.[18] Étienne Gilson summarizes the reasons why Ockhamism marks the end of the golden age of scholasticism. In theology, Ockham's doctrine paved the way for the "positive theology" of the moderns—that is, a study of the sources of theology—whereas in philosophy, Ockham paved the way for modern empiricism.[19] Neither development favors the achievement of Thomas Aquinas.

One emblematic event that signals the disintegration caused by various currents of fourteenth-century thought occurs at the start of the fifteenth century, when the Duke of Burgundy organized the murder of the French king's brother, Louis d'Orleans. In order to escape recrimination, the Burgundians engaged a professor, Master John Petit, to deliver in 1408 a public oration that aimed to justify, with some success, the cold-blooded political assassination. In order to bolster his arguments, John Petit availed himself of citations from Thomas Aquinas. What best illustrates, however, the "dangerous processes" in action appears in the rhetorical elaboration of Master Petit's four-hour discourse. According to one learned account, "the entire plea is artfully illustrated with scholastic distinctions and secondary texts."[20] In a remarkable triumph of style over substance, the achievement of the high scholastic period found itself suddenly put at the service of urban brigandry. Dominicans nonetheless remained active in Paris at the start of the fifteenth century, even though the French king Charles VI, whose brother was the victim of the Burgundians, displayed an uncharacteristic (for the French monarchy) disfavor toward the Dominicans at Saint-Jacques. Some wrongly thought that John Petit was a Dominican. In any event, the conventions of scholasticism had begun to leave a bad taste in some mouths of the Parisian intelligentsia.

---

18. See Josef Pieper, *Scholasticism: Personalities and Problems of Medieval Philosophy*, trans. Richard Winston and Clara Winston (New York: McGraw-Hill, 1964), 150.
19. Gilson, *History*, 498–99.
20. Johan Huizinga, *The Autumn of the Middle Ages*, trans. Rodney J. Payton and Ulrich Mammitzsch (Chicago: University of Chicago Press, 1996), 271.

Attacks and Defense

From the end of the fourteenth century, Paris had begun to grow cool toward Aquinas and his interpreters. Sometimes it happened that Aquinas's supporters failed to accomplish well their objectives. For instance, the Thomist position on the Immaculate Conception as defended in May 1387 by the Aragonese Dominican John de Monson galvanized the anti-Thomist party. Controversy erupted. The University of Paris itself turned against the Thomists.[21] In support of the university taking this position, Peter of Ailly (d. 1420), sometime chancellor of the university, recalled how many treatises written during the fourteenth century criticized Aquinas and his work, whereas John Gerson (d. 1429), who demonstrated a better attitude toward the scholastic style, lost patience with what he took as rhetorical excesses by pompous lecturers—presumably a reference to the inaugural lecture by John of Monson.[22] This historical incident may partly explain why interventions made against the Thomist teachings centered on questions of the divine omnipotence. Because the Thomists rejected Scotus's view that the fittingness and possibility of an immaculate conception suffices to explain Mary's grace, their critics accused them of limiting the exercise of divine power. Aquinas, on the other hand, preferred to place Mary's sanctification within the context of divine revelation and its account of salvation history. He accordingly shied away from unrevealed manifestations of God's omnipotence and maintained a discreet silence about any hypothetical ones. The anti-Thomist atmosphere evident at the start of the fifteenth century in Paris provides the backdrop for understanding the master work of a young Provençal Dominican who would come to occupy a premier place among the interpreters of Aquinas. In 1407, John Cabrol, known commonly as Capreolus, arrived in Paris to eventually teach the *Sentences*. He would have been cognizant of the shameful rhetoric of John Petit. One may also assume that he discovered no small amount of anti-Thomist affect distributed throughout the winding streets of the Latin Quarter.

John Capreolus (1380–1444) emerges out of the Dominican circles

---

21. For a detailed account of the intellectual context of Paris at the start of the fifteenth century, see Ruedi Imbach, "Le Contexte Intellectuel de l'Oeuvre de Capreolus" in *Jean Capreolus et son temps: 1380–1444*, ed. Guy Bedouelle, Romanus Cessario, and Kevin White, Mémoire Dominicaine (Paris: Les Éditions du Cerf, 1997), 13–22.
22. See Erika Rummel, *The Humanist-Scholastic Debate in the Renaissance and Reformation* (Cambridge, MA: Harvard University Press, 1995), 34–40.

active in fourteenth-century Toulouse. Born at Rodez, in the Rouergue region of Provençal France, Capreolus began his studies at the Toulouse Dominican *studium*.[23] As happened with Aquinas himself, the Dominicans took care to train their own new members within the rhythms of a proper conventual life. The young Capreolus obviously showed intellectual promise and was sent to Paris to complete his university training, which he did by 1412. Once arrived in Paris, Capreolus encountered the high-powered opposition voiced against the teaching of Aquinas. Peter of Ailly and John Gerson represented the modern way, the *via moderna*, which, in addition to countenancing the nominalism of Ockham, also found common cause with the new humanism that dawned in Europe at the end of the fourteenth century, especially in Italy with Francis Petrarca (d. 1374). In his *De Otio Religioso*, Petrarch, as he is known in English, immortalized the leisure that the religious enjoy for contemplation; he also made fashionable the study of humane letters (*litterae humanae*) based on the classics of antiquity. On the other hand, scholastic dialectics merited Petrarch's disdain: "You see how far things have gone: those who profess a knowledge of divine things have been transformed from theologians into dialecticians, not to say sophists."[24] Capreolus, as a quick glance at his Latin style indicates, remained undeterred by the humanist critique, while at the same time undertaking a strong rebuttal of the nominalist and other critics of Aquinas, including Durandus of Saint-Pourçain.

Capreolus deserves credit for his ingenuity. His *Defensiones theologiae divi Thomae Aquinatis*, which one authority translates as *Arguments in Defense of the Theology of Saint Thomas Aquinas*, represents "a highly-innovative contribution to the Parisian tradition of commentaries on the *Book of Sentences*."[25] The four books were completed at the Dominican priory in Rodez by early 1432. Because of his comprehensive defense of Aquinas's intellectual project, Capreolus occupies a position of primacy among the interpreters of Aquinas. In fact, since the fifteenth century, he has been known as their prince, *Princeps Thomistarum*. The regal title connotes the formative influence that Capreolus has exercised on the Thomist commentatorial tradition. He stands among those who follow him as prince but also as an exemplar for treating the thought of Aquinas as a unified expression of wisdom,

---

23. See Bernard Montagnes, "Le Midi dominicain au temps de Capreolus (1380–1450)," in Bedouelle, Cessario, and White, *Jean Capreolus et son temps*, 49–54.
24. Francis Petrarch to Francesco Nelli as cited in Rummel, *Humanist-Scholastic Debate*, 30.
25. Kevin White, "Translators' Introduction," in *On the Virtues*, by John Capreolus, ed. and trans. Kevin White and Romanus Cessario (Washington, DC: Catholic University of America Press, 2001), xxviii.

human and divine. Given the place and date of his birth (1380), it is not impossible that the young Capreolus inherited certain oral traditions about Aquinas and his intellectual achievement especially from Dominicans in the Midi of France. In any case, Capreolus exhibits an indefatigable confidence about the value of Aquinas's teaching for both the church and the Dominican Order, and he set about to ensure that Aquinas's positions were rightly promulgated. Toward this end, Capreolus applied himself to the Herculean task of setting the record straight. His *Defense* took on the major critics of Aquinas's way of thinking about things. Capreolus identified the authors who took exception to Aquinas's teaching and he remonstrated with them. These authors include not only people like Durandus of Saint-Pourçain but also John Duns Scotus; Peter Aureolus (d. 1322), a Franciscan who engaged both Aquinas and Scotus on the psychology of human knowledge; and Henry of Ghent (d. 1291), a contemporary of Aquinas who, for a time, rivaled him in popularity as a theologian. Although Capreolus died some years before the invention of the printing press, the *princeps* edition of his *Defensiones* appeared as early as 1483 (vols. 1–3) and 1484 (vol. 4). Extant copies of this edition suggest that it enjoyed wide circulation even during the "humanist" epoch.[26]

The achievement of Capreolus should not overshadow the accomplishments of other interpreters of Aquinas who flourished during the fifteenth century.[27] One notable figure among them emerges in the philosopher Dominic of Flanders (d. 1479), whose intellectual career revolves around the Dominican-rich territory of Bologna and Florence. For Flanders, Aquinas appears as the "Doctor sanctus" or the "Doctor gloriosus," appellations that suggest the revered place that Aquinas came to hold in the intellectual life of the Dominican Order and outside of it. Dominic of Flanders wrote more than what has survived of his work. His extant principal work, however, *Quaestiones in commentaria S. Thomae super* Metaphysicis *Aristotelis*, merits him his reputation as a leading and early interpreter of Aquinas's complete philosophical outlook. Flanders understood the internal coherence of the Thomist philosophical achievement, and so he criticized as eclectic those he considered Thomists in name but not in fact—"thomistae, nomine et non re."[28] Dominic of Flanders died in the Florence of Lorenzo de'

---

26. Guy Bedouelle, "Les Éditions 'Humanistes' de Capreolus," in Bedouelle, Cessario, and White, *Jean Capreolus et son temps*, 195–207.
27. For further information, see Serge-Thomas Bonino, "L'école thomiste au XVe siècle," *Rivista teologica di Lugano* 5 (2000): 223–34.

Medici, the Magnificent (d. 1492), who was close to the Dominicans. Earlier in the same city, which witnessed a renewal of the Dominican Order under the impulse of Blessed John Dominici (d. 1419), Antoninus of Florence (d. 1459) flourished as archbishop and moral theologian. The wide range of pastoral and practical questions that Antoninus addresses in his *Summa theologica moralis* shows the applicability of Thomist principles to circumstances such as the development of financial services and banking that Aquinas himself did not treat extensively. Antoninus considered himself a full-fledged Thomist and was not hesitant to make Aquinas's opinions his own.

Although the history of the growth of Thomist interpreters appears to track developments within the Dominican Order to which Aquinas belonged, the truth of the matter reveals a more complex pattern of development. Some fifty manuscripts remain from the fifteenth century by authors who were not Dominicans and who still treat Aquinas's theology and philosophy. Twenty or so of these scholars worked in Poland. Still, Dominicans corporately devoted themselves to the propagation of Aquinas's teaching. A figure such as Peter of Bergamo (d. ca. 1482), who held positions of responsibility for studies at Bologna, produced pedagogical tools that obviously demonstrate the comprehensive dimension that characterized the Dominicans' approach to Aquinas after Capreolus. Bergamo's *Tabula aurea*, a thematic overview of the complete works of Aquinas, enjoyed an early printing success at Bologna and Basle.[29] From the intellectual environment that Peter of Bergamo oversaw, gifted students, including Dominic of Flanders, arose who also promoted Aquinas's works. Paul Barbus Soncinas (d. 1494), for example, produced a commentary on Capreolus.[30] Soncinas also entertained discussions with Giovanni Pico della Mirandola (d. 1494), the eclectic humanist who nonetheless found a friend in the ill-fated reformer Jerome Savonarola (d. 1498). Ordinarily, one does not associate the Dominican Savonarola with the company of Thomists. However, the celebrated preacher of reform had studied Aquinas, in fact under Peter of Bergamo, and at the start of his priestly life also gave lessons in Thomist thought. More renowned as a preacher than

---

28. See Jörgen Vijgen, "Dominicus von Flandern," in *Thomistenlexikon*, ed. David Berger and Jörgen Vijgen (Bonn: Verlag Nova et Vetera, 2006), 150.
29. For a brief account, see George Tyrrell, "The 'Tabula Aurea' of Peter De Bergamo," *The Heythrop Journal* 10, no. 3 (1969): 275–79. Peter of Bergamo also composed a "Concordantiae Texuum discortantium Divi Thomae Aquinatis."
30. Paul Soncinas, *Epitoma quaestionum in IV libros senentiarum a principe Thomistarum Joanne Capreolo Tolesano disputatarum*, 1st printed ed. (Pavia, 1522).

as a professor, Savonarola found inspiration for his preaching, at least in part, from the biblical commentaries of Aquinas. The drama and political conflict that Savonarola's celebrated execution evokes should not obscure the significant advances that the followers of Aquinas achieved during the second half of the fifteenth century. Indeed, Savonarola, instead of overreaching himself, may have profited by paying attention to the equilibrium and serenity of Aquinas's approach to problems. At the end of an excruciating day, as one historian notes, "Savonarola's reform efforts were too mixed up with political contingencies and with an apocalyptic vision of an earthly kingdom of Christ."[31] Aquinas was too level-headed to allow such preoccupations and illusions to distract him from the pursuit of the *sacra doctrina*.

---

31. Guy Bedouelle, *The Reform of Catholicism: 1480-1620*, trans. James K. Farge (Toronto: Pontifical Institute of Medieval Studies, 2008), 17.

6

Expansion and Recognition

The Emergence of the *Summa theologiae*

The Belgian Peter Crockaert (d. 1514) holds a place of special importance among Thomists of the Renaissance period.¹ As a young man, Crockaert fell under the influence of well-known nominalist teachers at Paris, especially John Major (1467–1550). While already in his thirties, Crockaert joined the Dominican Order in Paris. His intentional embrace of the Dominican form of life led him to the Congregation of Holland, one of the organs of reform that had begun to flourish among the Dominicans.² One, of course, argues invalidly that what comes after an event follows causally upon it. At the same time, Crockaert, having taken up the rhythms of Dominican conventual life, did abandon his preference for nominalist philosophy and begin at Paris to teach the *Summa theologiae*. This work of Aquinas opens with a discussion of God as pure actuality.³ Architecture reflects styles of living and outlooks.

---

1. For a short overview of this period, written however from a perspective critical of the commentators, see Philippe Lécrivain, "La «Somme théologique» de Thomas d'Aquin aux XVIe–XVIIIe siècles," *Recherches de Science Religieuse* 91, no. 3 (2003): 397–427.
2. Reform among the Dominicans dates back to the fourteenth century. Raymund of Capua (d. 1399), who received inspiration from Catherine of Siena even as he directed her spiritual growth, inaugurated the reform movements. For further information, see William A. Hinnebusch, *The Dominicans: A Short History* (New York: Alba House, 1975), chapters 4–7. In 1515, Thomas de Vio, Cajetan, then master of the Order, turned the Congregation of Holland into a province.
3. See *Summa theologiae* 1a, q. 3, art. 3.

The monastic cloister that the classical Dominican priory incorporated into its structure leaves an open space at its center that directs the mind beyond the skies toward God. Crockaert's dramatic change of school allegiance also affords some glimpse of the swirling intellectual climate that enveloped centers of learning by the start of the sixteenth century.

Interest in the *Summa*, though not necessarily its adoption as a curriculum-shaping textbook, began to develop shortly after the death of John Capreolus in 1444. At Strasbourg, for instance, one printed edition of *Summa* questions, the *prima-secundae*, dates from before 1463.[4] This and other precedents during the last half of the fifteenth century indicate that Dominicans and other professors in Europe were teaching questions, at least, from the *Summa theologiae*.[5] Still, Peter Crockaert represents an important turning point in the Thomist commentatorial tradition. He marks a break with the time-honored preference for choosing the *Sentences* of Peter Lombard and commentaries on its four books, including that of Aquinas himself, as the ordinary vehicle for giving theological instruction. Instead, Aquinas's *chef d'oeuvre* begins to guide Catholic theology. The adoption of the *Summa* proceeds organically, however, that is, from professor to student. It took time, moreover, for some universities and schools to realize this change in preferred theology textbook. "At the University of Louvain," Torrell reports, "we will have to wait until 1596 for the *Summa* to replace the *Sentences* in its curriculum."[6] Historians of art like to compare Aquinas's *Summa* with the architecture of France's Gothic cathedrals, which reach their own highpoint during the thirteenth century. Both *Summa* and cathedral exhibit a well-ordered harmony of divine faith and human achievement.[7]

All in all, the sixteenth century witnesses a flourishing of the Thomist commentatorial tradition. One zenith occurs when Pope Pius V (d. 1572) on 11 April 1567 declares Aquinas a doctor of the church,

---

4. Jean-Pierre Torrell, *Aquinas's Summa: Background, Structure, and Reception*, trans. Benedict M. Guevin, OSB (Washington, DC: Catholic University of America Press, 2005), 93. For a detailed and scholarly account of the diffusion of Aquinas's *Summa theologiae* in manuscript or printed form, see ibid., 92–96.
5. Gilles Charronelle, a Dominican teaching at Paris, was Crockaert's teacher and used the *Summa theologiae*.
6. Torrell, *Aquinas's Summa*, 96.
7. See for example the ironical observation of Élie Faure in his *History of Art: Medieval Art*, trans. Walter Pach (New York: Harper, 1922), 338: "The cathedral, indeed the whole art of the ogive, realizes for a moment the equilibrium between the virgin forces of the people and the metaphysical monument whose mold Christian philosophy had been preparing for a thousand years. But these forces break the mold when they have attained their full expansion."

the first theologian after the patristic period to receive the title.[8] This honor did not emerge adventitiously. A stunning collection of Thomist authors, mainly though not exclusively Dominicans, adorn the intellectual landscape of the sixteenth century.

The figure who dominates the first decades of the sixteenth century appears in the person of Thomas de Vio, Cajetan, named after Gaeta, an important port city then located in the kingdom of Naples, where he was born on 20 February 1469. Still in his mid-teens, James de Vio received the name Thomas (as in Aquinas) when, in 1484, he entered the Dominican Order. This precocious young man progressed through the various stages of academic preparation that led to his receiving the highest credential in theology. In 1494, the young *magister* Cajetan famously disputed at Ferrara with Giovanni Pico della Mirandola, whom the Dominican preacher Jerome Savonarola (1452–1498) received into the Dominican Order as Pico della Mirandola lay close to death from poisoning later that same year.[9] These discussions exemplify the judicious way that Thomists engaged the humanist thinkers of the High Renaissance. Humanism, it is generally agreed, was typically a literary and educational movement. Most humanists showed a certain indifference toward philosophy.[10] Cajetan, on the other hand, enters the debate over the value of epideictic literature and shows the young Pico della Mirandola that his appreciation for words and rhetoric must lead him to embrace the truth they express.

None accuse Cajetan of imprecision in thought. At the same time, few observe how well he embodies the Thomist ideal that envisages the simultaneous pursuit of both the contemplative and the active lives. He followed the wise counsel of Aquinas, "just as it is better to illuminate than merely to shine, so it is better to give to others the things contemplated than simply to contemplate."[11] Cajetan paid a dear price for his choice of religious institutes. His recognized intellectual abilities did not guarantee Cajetan, even as a Dominican, the reclusive life of a university or *studium* professor. Instead, from the turn of the sixteenth century, he was obliged to fulfill administrative duties, first for the Dominican curia in Rome and then for the Holy See. In 1508, Caje-

---

8. See Nicole Lemaître, *Saint Pie V* (Paris: Fayard, 1994), 168.
9. William A. Hinnebusch, *The History of the Dominican Order*, vol. 1, *Origins and Growth to 1500* (New York: Alba House, 1965), 297.
10. For further information, see Erika Rummel, *The Humanist-Scholastic Debate in the Renaissance and Reformation* (Cambridge, MA: Harvard University Press, 1995), 41–62.
11. *Summa theologiae* 2a–2ae, q. 188, art. 6. Translation taken from Thomas Aquinas, *The Pastoral and Religious Lives*, ed. and trans. Jordan Aumann, vol. 47 (2a2ae. 183–89) of *Summa Theologiae* (London: Blackfriars, 1973), 205.

tan assumed the post of master of the Dominican Order. The remainder of his life, some twenty-six years, finds Cajetan occupied with affairs both political and theological. In 1517, the pope named Cajetan a cardinal. The next year, Cajetan met with Martin Luther in Germany as part of an unsuccessful attempt to respond to the latter's theological difficulties.

Cajetan reveals himself as the model of what a Catholic theologian should strive to attain. He demonstrates competence in philosophy, biblical studies, and sacred theology—the proverbial Renaissance man. It stands as a testimony to the devotion with which he pursued the Dominican ideal of study that he was able to compose his commentary on the three parts of the *Summa theologiae* between 1507 and 1522 while at the same time addressing difficult issues that confronted the church following the sixteenth-century reform movement known as Protestantism. He remained unswerving in his submission to the authority of Aquinas, as his reference to him as the "father of proper moral theology" indicates. We should follow Saint Thomas, bluntly insists Cajetan, not whomsoever may come along.[12] All in all, Cajetan penned more than one hundred different works. During the 1527 sack of Rome, the ransom set for the Dominican cardinal was the smallest exacted by the mutinous soldiers of the Hapsburg emperor, Charles V (d. 1558). In 1540, just six years after Cajetan's death in Rome, his commentary on the *Summa* appeared in print at Lyons.[13] For himself, the distinguished Cajetan chose an unadorned grave in the vestibule of Santa Maria *sopra* Minerva, the church in Rome where Dominicans still guard the body of Catherine of Siena.

Cajetan witnesses to the continuity of the Thomist commentatorial tradition. He obviously read Capreolus. At the same time, Cajetan's scholarly engagements reveal the malleability of the commentators. Some views that Cajetan held failed to gain widespread acceptance among other Thomist commentators, including both Cajetan's contemporaries and later Thomists. Change in the ambient intellectual culture obviously affects, to some degree, the way that Thomists discuss Aquinas's principles and conclusions. They want to not only shine but

---

12. See Cajetan's *Commentary* on *Summa Theologiae* 2a–2ae, q. 151, art. 4, no. 2: "Ad secundam obiectionem, ex Hugutionis auctoritate, dicitur quod, quia unaquaeque ars propriis terminis seu vocabulis gaudet, ideo nos in moralibus rectius moralium Patrem, divum Thomam, quam extraneum quempiam sequimur."
13. For a good bibliography of Cajetan's works, see Harm Klueting, "Thomas de Vio Cajetan," in *Thomistenlexikon*, ed. David Berger and Jörgen Vijgen (Bonn: Verlag Nova et Vetera, 2006), 71–78. The entry also includes a comprehensive list of secondary literature.

also illumine. Because Cajetan demonstrated, for example, a willingness to address the educated laymen of his day, he found himself sometimes at odds with those who had been formed in an earlier period when intellectual exchanges mainly transpired among clerics. Even those who had mastered John Capreolus grew impatient with Cajetan. For example, his elder brother in the Dominican Order, Silvester Mazzolini (1456–1527), better known as Prierias (after the obscure village of his birth, Prierio) exhibited antagonisms. This author of the popular summary of John Capreolus, *Epitome Capreoli* (1487), criticized Cajetan when he departed from what Prierias considered the received opinions of earlier Thomists.[14] Such fluctuations inevitably emerge when one examines seven centuries of a common tradition. The heavy-handed, historically minded scholar frets over minor discrepancies. The Thomist, on the other hand, marvels at the capacity that the works of Aquinas demonstrate to sustain a seven-hundred-year suite of non-eclectic commentators.[15] What characterizes the authentic evolution of the Thomist commentatorial tradition remains its adherence to the first principles of speculative thought, both in the natural and the supernatural orders. In other words, Thomists address the secular culture without capitulating to it. Like the evangelization of peoples, the Thomist task also presents its own challenges.

In the exchanges that Cajetan enjoyed with Pietro Pomponazzi (1462–1525), we see the celebrated Thomist fully engaged in high-level academic discussions of his period.[16] Even Homer nods, though. Cajetan "was led, probably by Averroistic influences, to doubt the conclusiveness" of the arguments that led to affirming the natural immortality of the soul.[17] One fellow Dominican, Bartholomew Spina (d. 1546), conspicuously took issue with Cajetan's views in his *De immortalitate animae*

---

14. For a strong presentation of the conflict between Prierias and Cajetan, see Michael Tavuzzi, "Capreolus dans les Écrits de Silvestro da Prierio, o.p. (1456–1527)," in *Jean Capreolus et son temps 1380–1444*, ed. Guy Bedouelle, Romanus Cessario, and Kevin White, Mémoire Dominicaine (Paris: Les Éditions du Cerf, 1997), 239–58; and Michael Tavuzzi, *Prierias: The Life and Works of Silvestro Mazzolini da Prierio, 1456–1527* (Durham, NC: Duke University Press, 1997).
15. For a discussion of the criteria for inclusion in the non-eclectic Thomist commentatorial tradition, see Romanus Cessario, *A Short History of Thomism* (Washington, DC: Catholic University of America Press, 2005).
16. For an overview of Pomponazzi's Aristotelian leanings, see Armand A. Maurer, *Medieval Philosophy: A History of Philosophy* (New York: Random House, 1962), 337–46. Maurer places Pomponazzi under the influence of the Aristotelian commentator, Alexander of Aphrodisias, instead of the better-known school of Averroism that dominated northern Italy by the end of the fifteenth century.
17. Benedict M. Ashley, *Theologies of the Body. Humanist and Christian* (Braintree, MA: The Pope John Center, 1985), 583 and also 170. "Averroistic influences" refers to the general intellectual climate that dominated secular learning in Italy at the turn of the sixteenth century. Cajetan and Pomponazzi, who was five years his senior, were colleagues at Padua and certainly encountered one another there.

(Venice, 1519). One of the signal examples of discrepancy in the Thomist commentatorial tradition, however, shows, in retrospect, how the tradition possesses the capacity to correct itself. Common Thomist opinion today holds that the immortality of the soul ranks among the *praeambula fidei*.[18] Criticism of another variety came to Cajetan from Ambrosius Catharinus de' Politi (1484–1553), a learned Dominican bishop who was present later at the Council of Trent. Catharinus, though more of a public intellectual than a Thomist, published his *Annotationes in Commentaria Cajetani super Sacram Scripturam* (Lyons, 1542). As the title of the work suggests, this confrere felt obliged to correct Cajetan's biblical exegesis, to which Cajetan devoted himself with vigor, especially after his encounter with Martin Luther. Still, the attention paid to Cajetan's *Commentary* on the *Summa* and its intrinsic worth even today guarantees him primacy of place within the Thomist commentatorial tradition.[19]

Cajetan's Colleagues

Francis Silvestri of Ferrara (1474–1528), also known as Ferrariensis, was a contemporary of Cajetan. Silvestri further illustrates the rich intellectual ambience that developed around Dominican foundations on the sixteenth-century Italian peninsula. The story goes that when Cajetan, while master of the Dominican Order, caught sight of Silvestri's commentary on the *Summa contra Gentiles*, he ordered its immediate publication. Silvestri followed the ordinary pattern of Dominican life: first he taught, then he administered, and he always preached. His other published works include commentaries on Aristotle's philosophical works and a devotional book on the life of a contemporary mystic, Blessed Osanna of Mantua (d. 1505). Silvestri's administrative skills enabled him to serve well as master of the Dominican Order. Travel became part of his ordinary routine, especially in France and the Duchy of Brittany. An overweight man, it is said, Silvestri died when a barge he was riding in capsized in the Vilaine River, which runs through the center of Rennes.

Silvestri remains the expert on the *Summa contra Gentiles*. Today, his

---

18. For further information on the preambles of faith, see Ralph McInerny, *Praeambula Fidei: Thomism and the God of the Philosophers* (Washington, DC: Catholic University of America Press, 2006).

19. In the twentieth century, it has become fashionable in some circles to accuse Cajetan of distorting Aquinas; however, these criticisms often reveal a failure to grasp his philosophical ingenuity. For example, see Steven A. Long, *Analogia Entis: On the Analogy of Being, Metaphysics, and the Act of Faith* (Notre Dame: University of Notre Dame Press, 2011).

commentary stands easily available in three volumes of the Leonine edition of Aquinas's works.[20] Although he made discreet criticisms of some of Cajetan's views, Francis Silvestri also demonstrated the highest respect for the Thomist commentator whose metaphysics exhibited a greater refinement of thought than his own. Still, scholars continue to examine the subtleties of Silvestri's own philosophical positions, especially his views on sensible knowledge, analogy, and individuation.[21] What is more important, Silvestri seems to have exemplarily shown how much theology needs philosophy in order to achieve its high objective of illuminating divine revelation. This respect for philosophy as essential to display the sacred sciences continues to characterize the Thomist commentatorial tradition.[22]

In Spain, Diego de Deza (ca. 1444–1523) claims renown for his association with the royalty of the Spanish lands where he was born about the same time as John Capreolus died in Provence. This Dominican bishop and statesman grasped the importance of Capreolus's *Defensiones* and tried to imitate them, especially in the composition of his own *In defensiones Sancti Thomae*, published at Seville in 1491. At about the same time, Deza was instrumental in gaining access to the Catholic monarchs, Ferdinand and Isabella, for the young Genovese navigator Christopher Columbus, whose discoveries made of this Dominican a first Thomist contact with the New World. Columbus himself testified that Deza made his voyages possible.[23] Deza's subsequent professional life concerns the religious and political life of the Iberian Peninsula after the relinquishment in 1492 of the sovereignty of the Moorish emirate of Granada to the Catholic monarchs of Spain. The *Reconquista* marks the beginning of a renewed political and religious order in Spain that would provide very suitable circumstances for the development of Thomist scholarship. When a young Spaniard, Francis de Vitoria (d. 1546), returned from Paris and the classroom of Peter Crockaert, where

---

20. In the nineteenth century, Pope Leo XIII ordered the commentary to be included in the new Leonine edition of Aquinas's works. See *Summa contra Gentiles*, vols. 13–15, *Sancti Thomae Aquinatis Opera omnia* (Rome, 1918–1926).
21. See the bibliographical information in Leo J. Elders, "Franciscus Sylvester von Ferrara," in Berger and Vijgen, *Thomistenlexikon*, 180–88. For an example of how Silvestri figures in one philosophical discussion, see Mark. K. Spencer, "The Personhood of the Separated Soul," *Nova et Vetera* 12, no. 3 (2014): 863–912.
22. For example, see the tribute to the work of Ralph McInerny: Matthew L. Lamb, ed., *Theology Needs Philosophy: Acting against Reason is Contrary to the Nature of God* (Washington, DC: Catholic University of America Press, 2016). For an introduction to the life and works of Aquinas that exposes his philosophical achievements, see James A. Weisheipl, *Friar Thomas D'Aquino: His Life, Thought, and Works* (Washington, DC: Catholic University of America Press, 1983).
23. For further information, see Pierre Mandonnet, *Les dominicains et la découverte de l'Amérique* (Paris: P. Lethielleux, 1893), 99–133.

they together edited the section of the *Summa* that treats the virtues, Vitoria profited from the royal support of higher learning. Around the University of Salamanca, there began a distinguished series of Spanish Thomists who, like Cajetan and Silvestri, have left a mark on Western intellectual history.

Francis de Vitoria, whose birth falls somewhere in the last two decades of the fifteenth century, gains recognition not only in theology and philosophy but also in the general areas of law and political science. Scholars recognize this Spanish jurist as one who contributed to the modern treatment of international law. Vitoria spent his first years as a Dominican in Paris, where he received his philosophical and theological training. As already mentioned, he sat in Peter Crockaert's classroom. Upon his return to Spain, and after a short stint of teaching at Valladolid, Vitoria moved to Salamanca, where he remained for the rest of his life. Caricatures of the Thomist commentatorial tradition sometimes suggest that those who inhabit it may display speculative acumen but little practical usefulness. Among the many possible rejoinders to such a superficial remark, one may point to the application that Francis de Vitoria makes of Thomist teachings to the vexing questions occasioned by the discovery of the New World and the people native to the American continent.[24] Vitoria certainly did not imagine a timeless universe; in fact, he rewrote his classroom lectures each year. This practice may explain why he never got around to publishing his compositions during his lifetime. Still, his influence through the publication of students' notes from his classes and the writings of his students themselves merit him a crucial place in the Thomist tradition. Vitoria emerges at an important juncture in Western history, namely the first decades of the early modern period. He died in 1546, after having refused on account of ill health an invitation to represent the Hapsburg emperor at the Council of Trent (1545–1563).

Capreolus's influence also appears in Germany. There, in 1476, Conrad Köllin was born at Ulm. This gifted young man entered the Dominicans, as was the custom of the time, while still in his teenage years, and during the period of his initial formation in the Order, he read and

---

24. See, for example, James B. Scott, preface to *Franciscus de Victoria de Indis et de Ivre Belli Reflectiones* (Washington, DC: Carnegie Institution, 1917): "Vitoria's claim as a founder of the Law of Nations must unfortunately be based upon these two readings taken down by a pupil and published after his death, without the professor's revision and in a very summary form. They are sufficient, however, to show that International Law is not a thing of our day and generation or of the Hague Conferences, nor indeed the creation of Grotius, but that the system is almost as old as the New World."

studied Capreolus. After further training in Heidelberg, Köllin took up the master's chair at Cologne in 1512 and so became the inheritor of a rich, though heterogeneous, intellectual tradition that dates back to Aquinas's own student years. Throughout the late fifteenth century, Thomism gained in popularity among the German Dominicans. Conrad Köllin develops out of this movement that gradually dominated over Albertism, an early-fourteenth-century philosophical venture that exhibits affinities with the *via moderna*.[25] He both taught the *Summa* and composed an exposition and commentary on the *prima-secundae* that was published in 1512 at Cologne. Scholars affirm that Köllin made fruitful use of the work of Capreolus, even though, as certain ones suggest, Köllin corrected alleged Augustinian readings of Aquinas that the Provençal Thomist had adopted.[26] Whatever the case may be, Köllin was no catalyst for the Reformation's notorious disdain for scholasticism. In fact, no evidence exists to prove that Luther ever read Köllin. In any event, the Reformation greatly curtailed the evolution of Thomism in Germany. By 1525, there were only twenty students in the Dominican *studium* at Cologne.[27] Köllin's achievement, however, represents a highpoint of Thomism in pre-Reformation Germany.

During the remainder of the fifteenth century, German Thomist authors turned to the pressing events of their day. By devising refutations, Dominicans such as Jerome Dungersheim (d. 1540) took up the battle against the emerging Lutheranism. He published his *Theorismata duodecim contra Lutheru[m]: quibus ex ipsiusmet dictis co[n]demnatur* at Leipzig in 1531. Principled rebuttal did not always work, however. Rhetors know that refutation poses the most difficult challenge to their art. Some observers suggest that "attacks on Luther seemed to persuade many that Luther's ideas might be worth considering . . . [and so] they elevated Luther in public opinion and gave him a wider audience."[28] In other words, rhetoric trumped reason. As one knowledgeable of the period observes, "[Philip] Melanchthon (1497–1560) produced a number of teaching texts in dialectic, coordinated with

---

25. This philosophical school of thought took up the teachings of Albert the Great, especially the Neoplatonic elements in his thought. It flourished in Cologne during the first decades of the fifteenth century but failed to establish there a lasting heritage. For further information, see Zénon Kaluza, "Les Débuts de L'Albertisme Tardif (Paris et Cologne)," in *Albertus Magnus und der Albertismus: deutsche Philosophische Kultur des Mittelalters*, ed. Maarten J. F. M. Hoenen and Alain de Libera (New York: Brill, 1995), 207–42.
26. See Denis R. Janz, *Luther and Late Medieval Thomism: A Study in Theological Anthropology* (Waterloo, ON: Wilfrid Laurier University Press, 1983), 102–10.
27. Ibid., 95.
28. Richard Marius, *Martin Luther: The Christian Between God and Death* (Cambridge, MA: Harvard University Press, 1999), 151.

his program for the humanist education of reformed Christians."[29] The humanist dialecticians gave up on arriving surely at truth. Instead they taught how to argue plausibly, with the result that they could easily create more doubt than certainty.

Spanish Thomists at the Council of Trent

During the sixteenth century, Dominicans, especially in Italy and Spain, supplied the largest number of authors who carried forward the commentatorial tradition centered on the writings of Thomas Aquinas. However, other mendicants, such as friars of the Augustinian and Carmelite orders, also contributed to the commentatorial tradition, as did, during the second half of the century, the Jesuits, who were founded in 1540. In fact, Saint Francis Borgia (d. 1572), before he became father general of the Jesuits, composed his *Praecipuae divi Thomae materiae*, published at Valencia in 1550. Additionally, professors without affiliation to a religious order, though often clerics, published commentaries and compendia or epitomes of Aquinas's works. One illuminating example comes from the pen of Bernard Bongean (Bonjoannes) (1538–1607), a bishop who published his *Epitome in Summa Theologiae* at Venice in 1564. This volume was available in English translation in nineteenth-century New York City.[30]

In those lands where the various branches of the Protestant reform took hold, Catholic theology moved in new directions. The reformers generally regarded the earliest expressions of institutional Christianity as perversions of the original biblical message. How much more would they not hold suspect the thirteenth-century thought of Thomas Aquinas? Scholasticism, it was generally held, distorts gospel truth more than explicates it. As it happened, however, the first Protestant divines were trained in the same school tradition as their Catholic counterparts. Some thought, perhaps paradoxically, that the *Loci communes* of Philip Melanchthon, first published in 1521, would serve as a kind of new *Summa*.[31] It did, but for Lutheranism. The author kept medieval Aristotelianism to a minimum.[32] Protestant scholastics rep-

---

29. Lisa Jardine, "Humanism and the Teaching of Logic," in *The Cambridge History of Later Medieval Philosophy*, ed. Norman Kretzmann, Anthony Kenny, and Jan Pinborg (Cambridge: Cambridge University Press, 1982), 801.
30. Berardus Bonjoannes, *Compendium of the Summa Theologica of St. Thomas Aquinas: Pars Prima*, ed. Wilfrid Lescher (New York: Benziger Brothers, 1906).
31. Philip Melanchthon, *Loci communes rerum theologicarum seu hypotyposes theologicae* (Wittenberg, 1521). For further discussion, see Ulrich G. Leinsle, *Introduction to Scholastic Theology*, trans. Michael J. Miller (Washington DC: Catholic University of America Press, 2010), 260.

resent discontinuity. As Erika Rummel observes about the early sixteenth century: "The humanists, for some time stereotyped as poets and grammarians meddling in theology, were now often labeled Lutherans; the scholastics, stereotyped as barbarians and quibblers, were now perceived as reactionary papists and corrupters of the true Church of Christ."[33] It comes as no surprise to learn that the Reformation quarrels eventually required a political resolution to settle them, as it were.[34]

The destruction of the mediating institutions of medieval Catholicism, mainly though not exclusively instantiated in monasteries, religious orders, and the universities, wreaked havoc on the intellectual life of Catholic Europe. Some may view these historical circumstances as felicitous opportunities for the advancement of humanist and scientific studies that continued to develop outside of strict ecclesiastical control. Only blind prejudice—something like an intellectual version of the Black Legend—would argue that the development of human knowledge would have been impeded by preserving the measured faith and reason interplay that characterized both the cathedrals and the universities of the High Middle Ages. The political fallout of the Reformation, especially the series of religious wars waged in Europe, caused much harm to the Thomist commentatorial tradition. The social and material supports that enabled Thomas Aquinas and his followers to work tranquilly were swept away in those places where the Reformation gained legitimacy. This destruction occurred mainly but not exclusively in the German states. France also suffered under the French Wars of Religion (1562–1598). In England, the political imposition of a state church as well as the emergence of dissenters from it practically eliminated a Thomist culture that dated back to Aquinas's own lifetime. The Dominicans were expelled abruptly from Oxford in 1538 and did not return as a group until the 1920s.

In Catholic lands, however, Thomists continued to flourish. Dominic de Soto emerges as a representative figure of Hapsburg Thomists.[35] He served as the father confessor to the emperor, Charles V. Born in 1494 at Segovia, Soto joined the Dominicans at the age of thirty, after

---

32. See Rummel, *Humanist-Scholastic Debate*, 168.
33. Ibid., 8.
34. A first instance occurs at the Peace of Augsburg in 1555, when Catholic and Lutheran factions settled for the principle that later became known as "cuius regio, eius religio" (whose realm, his religion). Later, in 1648, the Treaties of Westphalia brought an end to the wars of religion.
35. For information on his life, see Vicente Beltran de Heredia, *Domingo de Soto: Estudio biográfico documentado* (Madrid: Ediciones Cultura Hispánica, 1961).

completing his studies at both Alcalá and Paris. He immediately took up teaching at the Dominican *studium* at Salamanca, Saint Stephen's, where he eventually replaced his older confrere, Francis de Vitoria. Since Vitoria was impeded from traveling, the emperor sent Soto as his representative to the Council of Trent, where he took part in the discussions about the Bible, grace, and scholastic theology. Soto's involvement in the ecclesiastical and political business of the day kept him away from teaching until 1552, when he returned to his chair of theology at Salamanca. Soto ranks among the great figures of this university. He stands out among Thomists for his defense of scholastic theology against those ecclesiastics who conceived the startling proposal to impose on religious monks and nuns the study of the Bible even to the point of eliminating instruction in scholastic theology. Soto's works include courses on much of the philosophical curriculum of the day, theological treatises (including his commentary on the four books of the *Sentences*), and special lectures (*relectiones*) given alongside his regular classroom instruction. Soto also engaged in a series of polemical exchanges, including with the Italian Dominican bishop and theological wildcard Ambrosius Catharinus.

Although the Spanish monarchs did everything to protect Spain from the encroachments of Lutheranism and its allied movements, certain reformers' views nonetheless made their way especially into centers of intellectual life. This infection mainly took the form of an Erasmian spirituality that gave preference to personal experience over external authority. The *alumbrados* (the illuminated ones) gained standing as a recognized group. Even Saint Ignatius Loyola, suspected of illuminism, was detained in 1527 for a short time by the Inquisition. The Dominican archbishop of Toledo, Bartholomew Carranza, fared less well. After Carranza fell under the Inquisition's charge of holding Lutheran sympathies, he spent nearly the last twenty years of his life under house arrest. Soto, who was close to his fellow Dominican, was saddened by the unfortunate series of events that plagued the archbishop, especially because Soto believed that he himself had furnished the Inquisition with certain inculpating critiques. The complex affair shows that Lutheran notions had probably crept into even honest efforts to present authentically the Catholic faith, such as Carranza's *Commentaries on the Christian Catechism*, published at Antwerp in 1558. The prolonged investigation of Carranza and his eventual acquittal on the major charges brought against him also give some indication of the confusions that large-scale departures from the church's teaching authority caused in Europe, especially throughout the sixteenth and seventeenth centuries. Soto himself died a holy death in November 1560. His student, Dominic Báñez, was present at his deathbed and reported that he witnessed signs of Soto's predestination in his holy manner of dying. Though Soto holds a larger-than-life status among Habsburg Thomist theologians, his student Báñez enjoyed a name recognition greater than that of his teacher. Still, Soto's reputation for learning earned him the sobriquet, "Qui scit Sotum, scit totum" (the one who knows Soto, knows everything).

Melchior Cano, though fifteen years Soto's junior, died the same year, 1560. A grave illness befell Cano on his way back from Rome, where he had gone in the hopes of receiving from Pope Pius IV confirmation of his election as the head of Spanish Dominicans, a post that had been denied him by the pope's predecessor. Like his elder brothers, Vitoria and Soto, Cano's life reflects the intense spiritual and intellectual energy that Catholic Spain generated during the sixteenth century. Cano contributed to the deliberations of the Council of Trent. Unlike the other two Thomists, Cano's publications arise exclusively from his lecturing in theology. He authors neither philosophy texts nor treatises on justice and social problems. Cano held what Thomists today would consider an eccentric position on the causality of the sacraments. At the same time, he also displays—one may opine—the elasticity of the Thomist commentatorial tradition. Of course, as happened with Cajetan's views on the natural immortality of the soul, Cano's thesis that defends the moral causality of the sacraments has not survived as the representative Thomist position. In fact, Cano's own student, Dominic Báñez, exposed the deficiencies of this, perhaps, humanist deviation from the classical teaching on the physical causality or instrumentality that works in the seven sacraments.[36]

Angelo Walz, OP, (1893–1978), a noteworthy twentieth-century historian, has written on the participation of Dominicans in the Council of Trent.[37] Dominicans occupied Trent even before the council. In the sixteenth century, in fact, the priory of Saint Lawrence (S. Lorenzo) at Trent flourished as a center of Dominican life. Although the conventual buildings were razed after the Second World War, some physical evidence remains of the rich library holdings of this convent. The list of Dominicans who participated in one way or another in the delib-

---

36. For further information, see Reginald M. Lynch, "Domingo Bañez on Moral and Physical Causality: Christic Merit and Sacramental Realism," *Angelicum* 91, no. 1 (2014): 105–25.
37. Angelo Walz, *I Domenicani al Concilio di Trento* (Rome: Herder, 1961).

erations of the Council of Trent include seven archbishops, six from Italy and one from Portugal; twenty-four bishops, representing a selection of European countries; two masters of the Dominican Order; eight official representatives (procurators) of bishops; and ninety-four theologians, many of them from Spain (*Hispanus*). In addition to those Thomists mentioned above as participants in the Tridentine deliberations, other Dominicans of the period who were present benefited from the same theological formation, especially in Italy and Spain.

Consider one example. Sent by Pope Pius IV to the third session of the council (1562–1563), Peter de Soto (1500–1563), a Spaniard, was occupied with the same range of political and theological endeavors in which Dominic de Soto and Cano engaged. More of an apologist than a Thomist, he nonetheless introduced in the mid-1550s the *Summa theologiae* as the major theology textbook at Dillingen in Swabia, where the prince-bishop of Augsburg had founded a school for the training of clerics. Peter de Soto went on to support the Catholic cause in England where, in fact, he sojourned for a while after the marriage on 25 July 1554 of Mary Tudor to Philip II of Spain, son of Charles V. The Spanish monarchy sent religious to England to help restore the Catholic Church. Indeed, Peter de Soto taught at Oxford and Cambridge during the reign of Queen Mary (1553–1558).[38] Tainted by the Carranza affair, however, controversy eventually engulfed Peter de Soto, who died before he could depart from Trent.

It has been said that the *Summa theologiae* was kept next to the Bible on the altar of the place where the fathers of Trent convened. This legend may have developed from a remark made by one of the Spanish bishops, who indicated that he had a copy of the *tertia pars* in his quarters. At the same time, as Walz observes, "the authority of Saint Thomas has no need of legends. At Trent, Aquinas supplied a first-class authority for both theologians and the Fathers. He would remain such for the post-Tridentine Church."[39] When the Dominican Michael Ghislieri ascended to the chair of Peter in 1566 as Pope Pius V, the work of implementing the reforms of the Council of Trent began in earnest. By the time of his death in 1572, Pius oversaw the apparatus of reform, especially the Roman Catechism. He renewed the structures of reform, which included both the visible organs of ecclesiastical governance and the instruments of invisible grace, such as the sacraments. This pope also gave his blessing to the first of the new religious orders of men and

---

38. Benedict M. Ashley, *The Dominicans* (Collegeville, MN: Liturgical Press, 1990), 131.
39. Walz, *Domenicani*, 314–15.

women who would become some of the principle Catholic agents after Trent.[40]

There exists no strict equipollency between the growth of Catholicism after the sixteenth century and the spread of Thomism. At the same time, as the presence of Thomists in influential positions at the Council of Trent suggests, anyone who wanted to exegete the main dogmatic definitions contained in the *Decrees* of the council would have had to consult Aquinas, especially his *Summa theologiae*. Further, as textual evidence confirms, the *Summa theologiae* accompanied the Catholic missionaries to the new lands that opened up as a result of exploration by the European powers. The Dominican Bartholomew of Ledesma (d. 1604), a bishop in Panama and Mexico, published his *De septem sacramentis* in Mexico City in 1556. During the first three-quarters of the sixteenth century, because of the recognition given to Aquinas, the Thomist commentatorial tradition achieves a certain coalescence. "The theological authority of Thomas was . . . enhanced," writes William A. Hinnebusch, "by the attention paid to his teaching at the Council of Trent, by Pius V's declaring him a Doctor of the Church in 1567, and the publication of the first complete printed edition of his works, the so-called Piana edition."[41] Among Dominicans, the writings of Aquinas received special commendation. From 1574, the Order required its theologians to take an oath to uphold his solid doctrine, a practice that lasted about four hundred years. Today, Dominicans receive warm encouragement: *lege Thomam!*

---

40. For further information on these agents of post-Tridentine reform, see Guy Bedouelle, *The Reform of Catholicism: 1480–1620*, trans. James K. Farge (Toronto: Pontifical Institute of Medieval Studies, 2008), 80–124.
41. Hinnebusch, *Dominicans*, 116.

7

Catholic Champions

Thomists Face Modernity

Jacques Maritain, in his essays in *Three Reformers*, explains the ruptures—religious, represented by Martin Luther (d. 1546), philosophical, by Rene Descartes (d. 1650), and moral, by Jean-Jacques Rousseau (d. 1778)—that affected European life from the beginning of the sixteenth century.[1] During this period of some 230 years, Lutheranism, Cartesianism, and Rousseauistic ideals each proposed casts of thought that led away from the principles that both undergird and sustain the teaching of Thomas Aquinas. Maritain's essays, in fact, criticize from a Thomist perspective the revolutionary religious, philosophical, and moral outlooks generated by these three diverse harbingers of modernity. Other recognized Thomists also have pointed out the dramatic differences between the thought of Aquinas and the modern philosophical temper. To cite one example, Étienne Gilson defends Thomist realism against the postulates of post-Cartesian epistemologies.[2] Noteworthy to observe, these twentieth-century critics have earned posthumous recognition from ecclesiastical authority.[3] What is most important to

---

1. See Jacques Maritain, *Three Reformers: Luther, Descartes, Rousseau* (New York: Crowell, 1970), 4.
2. See Étienne Gilson, *Thomist Realism and the Critique of Knowledge*, trans. Mark A. Wauck (San Francisco: Ignatius Press, 1986).
3. For instance, see John Paul II, *Fides et Ratio*, no. 74.

remember is that from the mid-sixteenth century through the end of the eighteenth century, Thomists sustained a framework for Catholic theology that has not lost its usefulness. Otherwise put, Thomist commentators and authors flourished alongside the new intellectual movements that dominated Europe during the early modern period.

Both the politics and the cultural achievements of the early modern period reveal that religion and theology did not disappear in the wake of advances in both science and overall secular enlightenment. The Iberian Thomist, John of St. Thomas, began to publish his multivolume *Cursus theologicus*, a commentary on the *Summa* of Aquinas, in 1637, the same year that René Descartes published his *Discourse on the Method*. Dominicans and members of other established religious orders, especially in France and Spain, played a major role in upholding what, in retrospect, one may consider a countercultural movement. In other words, the commentatorial tradition did not suffer eclipse with the advent of modernity. On the contrary, the Thomist commentatorial tradition figured prominently wherever Catholicism flourished or was implanted for the first time. As they have done since the thirteenth century, interpreters of Aquinas have put his thought to the service of the truth of the Catholic faith. In the twentieth century, a Jesuit theologian clearly expressed the service that Aquinas renders to truth seeking: "By the very fact of anyone embracing the doctrine of St. Thomas, he embraces the doctrine most commonly accepted in the Church, safe and approved by the Church itself."[4]

Once the Society of Jesus began to flourish as an instrument of Catholic reform, their scholarly members joined the expository class of Thomists. Sometimes disagreements arose between the established carriers of the tradition and these new clerk regular, the Jesuits. Saint Ignatius conceived of his company as a group of soldiers always ready for engagement. Jerome Nadal (d. 1580), one of their own and an early influence on the Jesuits, described them as contemplatives in action.[5] As part of the Catholic response to Protestantism, the Jesuits became accustomed to engaging the frontiers of evangelization, whether the

---

4. Joseph de Guibert, *De Ecclesia Christi* (Rome: Università Gregoriana, 1929), 386, as cited in Santiago Ramírez, "The Authority of St. Thomas Aquinas," *The Thomist* 15, no. 1 (1952): 109.
5. In Nadal's own words: "Father Ignatius enjoyed this kind of prayer by reason of a great privilege and in a most singular manner, and this besides, that in all things, actions, and conversations he contemplated the presence of God and experienced the reality of spiritual things, so that he was a contemplative likewise in action (a thing which he used to express by saying: God must be found in everything.)" For a full reference, see Joseph Conwell, *Contemplation in Action: A Study in Ignatian Prayer* (Spokane, WA: Gonzaga University, 1957), 25. For further information, see John P. McIntyre, *Gli* Esercizi spirituali *di Ignazio di Loyola* (Milan: Jaca Book, 1998).

peripheries were geographical or intellectual ones. It is therefore fair to generalize that Jesuit Thomists tended to keep an eye on the currents of early modern philosophy more than did most other Thomists. Indeed, some rapprochements with modernity disposed Jesuits to make accommodations in the philosophical and theological principles that the established commentatorial tradition did not judge opportune or even legitimate. In order to make allowances for commentators who followed Aquinas in a highly personalized way, scholars, as already noted, speak about eclectic Thomists.[6] Even with this distinction and the variety of views that Thomists expressed on a number of theological issues, it is a remarkable thing that Thomists carried on a lively intellectual existence that ran parallel to the upstart Protestant and secular initiatives. Bright Thomists, for the most part Catholic clerics, successfully navigated the ideological changes that Europe absorbed between 1517, when Luther protested against Johann Tetzel (the Dominican preacher of indulgences), and the eighteenth century, at least until the assault on the Bastille in Paris in 1789. This period includes the whole of the seventeenth century, which witnessed significant advances in scientific experimentation and learning. Throughout this period, Thomist authors maintained a commentatorial tradition that effectively shaped Catholic theology and the influence that it exercised outside of church venues.

The Catholic reform arrived later in France than in other places of Europe.[7] The flourishing of post-Tridentine initiatives followed a tumultuous period of civil discord in *la belle France* known as the French Wars of Religion (1562–1598). However, an informative study of seventeenth-century France maintains that despite the fire and ashes that characterized the late sixteenth-century civil conflict in France, "so much of the energy and initiatives for religious change at work during the early part of the seventeenth century were rooted in the experiences of those earlier decades."[8] Seventeenth-century France, especially in light of the seventy-two year reign of the French Sun King, Louis XIV (1643–1715), became a rich seedbed both for renewal of the

---

6. James A. Weisheipl, "Thomism," in *Catholic Encyclopedia*, vol. 14, *Simony-Tournély*, ed. Charles G. Herbermann (New York: Robert Appleton Company, 1912), 698.
7. Nonetheless, the extensive literary output of the Dominican apologist Pierre Doré (d. 1559), as one historian points out, "made some of Aquinas' insights accessible in French and in summary form to a theologically uneducated public." For further information, see John Langlois, *A Catholic Response in Sixteenth-Century France to Reformation Theology: The Works of Pierre Doré* (Lewiston, NY: Edwin Mellen Press, 2003).
8. Joseph Bergin, *Church, Society, and Religious Change in France 1580-1730* (New Haven: Yale University Press, 2009), 3.

church and for development of Thomist theology. At the same time, France followed her own political objectives within Europe.

The Thirty Years' War (1618–1648) pitted a coalition of Protestant powers against the Catholic countries, except France, which sided with the Protestants as a way of putting a check on Hapsburg hegemony throughout Europe. Hostilities came to an end with the Treaties of Westphalia (1648–1649). As a result of this "Peace of Westphalia," confessional differences were acknowledged as settled features of the European political landscape. The popes protested the arrangements, which gave political legitimacy to the several Protestant denominations (e.g., in the Calvinist Lowlands and Lutheran Sweden). Nonetheless, "Christianity according to the medieval ideal had," as one scholar admits, "disappeared."[9] The thought of Thomas Aquinas, however, survived, even in countries with divided confessional allegiances, such as Holland and Germany. The lands ruled by the Hapsburgs, whose boundaries stretched from Portugal to Prague and from Brussels to Palermo, provided especially fertile ground for the development of the Thomist commentatorial tradition. As did France, the other major European Catholic power of the early modern period, even though her balance-of-power politics made for some unlikely alliances.

Moral Theology

Survival does not mean ossification. One area where Thomists adopted perspectives that did not cohere fully with the classical form of their discipline involves the treatment of moral theology. From the middle of the sixteenth century, Catholic moral theology took a turn toward moral casuistry.[10] Instead of teaching ethics according to the received plan of the virtues, gifts, and Beatitudes, moral theologians began to rely for direction on the opinions held by learned men. Pascal famously parodied this new school of moral casuistry, which takes its name from its focus on figuring out right conduct for given cases (in Latin, *casus*).[11] Nonetheless, moral casuistry would enjoy about a four hundred year reign. Since the shift of paradigms became part of everyday Catholic life, especially with the renewal of the sacrament of penance after the

---

9. Guy Bedouelle, *The History of the Church* (London: Continuum, 2003), 109.
10. For a discussion of the evolution of moral casuistry in the sixteenth century, see Servais Pinckaers, *The Sources of Christian Ethics*, trans. Sr. Mary Thomas Noble (Washington, DC: Catholic University of America Press, 1995); and Romanus Cessario, *Introduction to Moral Theology*, rev. ed. (Washington, DC: Catholic University of America Press, 2013).
11. See Blaise Pascal, "Fifth Letter Written to a Provincial by One of His Friends," in *The Provincial Letters*, trans. A. J. Krailsheimer (Baltimore: Penguin Books, 1967), 74–87.

Council of Trent, Thomists, of course, followed the new casuist paradigm for moral theology. Moral science, when applied to a particular set of circumstances and problems, does not attain to a degree of demonstrative certitude. Too many variables can arise. In addition, opinions can vary. Schools of casuist opinion, in which acknowledged specialists were grouped together according to their general outlook on how to apply moral laws to specific cases, gradually developed.

Four main schools of casuistry may be cited: tutiorism, laxism, probabilism, and probabiliorism. Some moralists held for a strict application of ethical guidelines no matter what incongruities a particular case might involve. These rigorists—or tutiorists, as they also were known—preferred to stay on the safe (*tutus*) side. Others, laxists, preferred to apply norms loosely, even to the point of abetting moral indulgence. Because concrete human conduct is subject to contingencies and variations, the opinions of even moderate experts—that is, those who espouse neither laxism nor rigorism—can differ. Opinions such as these are known as probable opinions. Aquinas himself discusses probable opinions when he treats how to evaluate evidence in a courtroom trial.[12] He, however, did not make learned opinions as such the basis for his overall moral teaching. Thomist moral theology maintains the unity of being and goodness. It develops around a teleology of the good—that is, of perfective ends for human life—not from a calculation about what experts hold about the pursuit of the good.

By the mid-sixteenth century, the paradigm shift in morals had taken hold of all Catholic moral teaching and practice. Thomists dealt with this evolution, which, as we have said, lasted until the mid-twentieth century. Their first attempts produced some misunderstandings. Take, for example, the case of Bartholomew of Medina (1528–1580), a Spanish Dominican, who at Salamanca succeeded in obtaining the main chair in theology.[13] He is thought to have proven himself a zealous though unique interpreter of Aquinas. His commentaries on the *Summa Theologiae* achieved international renown as witnessed by the many editions of his works published all over Europe: Salamanca, of course, but also Venice, Cologne, Bergamo, Como, Saragossa, and Barcelona. Unfortunately, however, his memory survives not because of his commentaries but because of a mistake. Students of moral theology encounter the name of Bartholomew of Medina because of the asso-

---

12. See *Summa theologiae* 2a–2ae, q. 70, art. 2.
13. For a general discussion of the university at Salamanca and its professors, see Juan Belda Plans, "Hacia Una Noción Crítica de la 'Escuela de Salamanca,'" *Scripta Theologica* 31, no. 2 (1999): 367–411.

ciation that later, in 1659, was made between Jesuit probabilism and Medina's theory of a probable opinion.[14] In reality, however, the effort to make this Dominican Thomist the originator of a very controversial piece of seventeenth-century moral casuistry fails. Medina was a moral theologian of the teleological good, not of the arguably licit. Truth to tell, he was drawn posthumously into the fray over probabilism that so exercised Pascal.[15]

In his own writings, Medina admitted that one may choose between two probable opinions that conclude differently about the variables involved in human action. Still, he insists that each opinion should adhere equally to the moral good—that is, each must embody the truth about the good of the human person. In other words, he acknowledged that good men can arrive at different sound solutions to concrete moral problems. Probabilism, by contrast, describes a school of thought where one may choose a course of action that may not embody the best moral advice, even though some arguments probably can be made to rescue the opinion from being dubbed completely laxist. Mainline Thomists avoided the risks involved in probabilism by insisting that when confronted with the moral question—namely, "What am I to do?"—the best advice lies in the majority of opinions rendered by recognized scholars. That is, the *more* probable opinion, as it was known, stands the best chance of guiding persons to the good. During the period of casuistry, this school of thought became known as probabiliorism. Bartholomew of Medina undoubtedly would have been surprised to discover that his commentary on the *prima-secundae* was, as it were, hijacked and, perhaps, even used on occasion to justify moral expediency. Otherwise put, Medina did not advance the view that the choice of an expedient solution can trump the pursuit of moral excellence as long as someone comes up with a probable opinion to support a person's following the course of action. In other words, he is not the father of casuist probabilism. Pascal, moreover, was correct to recognize in the arguments of the probabilists a diversion from sound Catholic thinking.

---

14. Scholars attribute this false association to the Jesuit polemicist Étienne Dechamps (d. 1701) in his *Quaestio facti. Utrum theologorum societatis Jesus propriae sint istae sententiae duae: prima, ex duabus opinionibus probabilibus possumus sequi minus tutam; secunda, ex duabus opinionibus probabilibus licitum est amplecti minus probabilem* (Paris: S. Cramoisy, 1659).

15. Pascal, "Thirteenth Letter to the Reverend Jesuit Fathers," in *Provincial Letters*, 193–206, esp. 206: "since your Probabilism makes the sound opinions of some of your authors useless to the Church, ... they only serve to show us by their contradictions the duplicity in your hearts."

Grace and Freedom

Thomists recognize that to elaborate a proper moral theology requires their making assertions about a preethical anthropology. Created human nature and its capacities figure prominently in Thomist accounts of moral theology, even when nature and its capacities are elevated to the new life of divine grace. Questions arise: what distinguishes the rational creature from infra-rational ones? What is human freedom? How does God influence our free choices? How does the human creature attain his final destiny, which is at once God's gift and the creature's work? The answer to these questions requires a proper understanding of the human person who, by faith and sacraments, becomes inserted into the drama of Christian salvation. After the Reformation, Thomists took up these matters in dialogue with both Protestant and other Catholics who debated the dynamics of salvation. In fact, by the seventeenth century, one of the main disputes that engaged Thomists involved Reformation-inspired quarrels about the workings of divine providence and human freedom. The disputes arose in part because of the density of the matter involved. One need only recall the opening prayer of the poet John Milton's *Paradise Lost*: "what in me is dark / Illumine, what is low raise and support; / That, to the highth of this great argument, / I may assert Eternal Providence, / And justify the ways of God to men."[16] Because of the English reformation, no English baroque Thomists developed. One may only imagine what contributions they would have made to the development of the commentatorial tradition. The blind Calvinist poet, however, was far from being the only thinker to vex over God's justice and man's lot.

On the Continent, Thomists took on the question of human freedom and eternal salvation within the general context of discussions about predestination. Lutheranism and Calvinism prompted some Catholic thinkers, including the chimerical Ambrosius Catharinus, to react in a directly opposite fashion from those Reformers who made predestination a double act of the divine will that rescued some persons from sin and damnation and passed by the rest. These controversial Catholic thinkers self-consciously abandoned the classical teaching that had come down from Saint Augustine and Saint Thomas in favor of following what one may describe—for that period—as new directions in theology. Generally speaking, such innovations prompted misunder-

---

16. John Milton, *Paradise Lost*, bk. 1, ln. 22–26.

standings about human autonomy. Additionally, they exaggerated the abilities of the human person unaided by divine grace. During the early modern period, grace-and-freedom debates dominated nearly two centuries of Catholic theological exchange and pastoral practice. By the start of the seventeenth century, the pope himself felt it necessary to intervene.

Catholic Spain gave rise to the dispute among Catholics. During the 1580s, a series of university exchanges raised questions about the metaphysical requirements for the exercise of human freedom. Those who favored the new directions argued that in order to exercise true created freedom, the human being must discover a neutral strip, a space free from divine intervention, that would afford the shining exercise of creaturely human willing. Unfortunately, according to the Thomists, the search for this neutral ground proves illusory. There does not exist a No Man's Land between God and the human creature. "Elsewise," as one scholar points out, "finite human creatures [would] roam the earth creating *ex nihilo* the added perfection or reality of their free determinations, entirely outside of the divine causality and the divine providence."[17] Still, as Aquinas emphasizes, human persons "are moved as instruments by God, yet in such a way as not to rule out our own self-motion through free choice."[18] The discussions about grace and freedom attracted many participants. Most famous among them remains the Jesuit thinker Louis de Molina, who in 1588 published at Lisbon his *Concordia liberi arbitrii cum gratiae donis*.[19]

One figure enjoys the best reputation for his rendering of the Thomist response to Molinist views on human freedom in concord with divine grace. He is Dominic Báñez (1528–1604), a Spanish Dominican whose career suggests the brilliance Thomism achieved on the Iberian Peninsula: studies at Salamanca, entrance into the Dominican Order, further philosophical and theological studies under the masters of the period, and teaching stints at Salamanca and later Ávila, where he served as a spiritual director for Teresa of Jesus, the Carmelite doctor of the church. After receiving his doctorate in 1565, Báñez started another round of teaching in the great universities and study centers of sixteenth-century Spain: Alcalá (near Madrid), Ávila, Salamanca,

---

17. Steven A. Long, "Providence, Freedom, and Natural Law," *Nova et Vetera* 4, no. 3 (2006): 562.
18. *Summa theologiae* 1a-2ae q. 21, art. 4, ad 2. Translation taken from Thomas Aquinas, *Principles of Morality*, ed. and trans. Thomas Gilby, vol. 18 (1a2ae. 18–21) of *Summa Theologiae* (London: Blackfriars, 1966), 119.
19. For further discussion, see Romanus Cessario, "Molina and Aquinas," in *A Companion to Luis de Molina*, ed. Matthias Kaufmann and Alexander Aichele (Leiden: Brill, 2013), 291–323.

Valladolid. He enjoyed standing in the Inquisition, wrote commentaries on the parts of the *Summa theologiae*, and served as an advisor to the Spanish king Philip II. All in all, he was a model Thomist during the high period of the Hapsburg baroque.

Dominic Báñez has earned a place in the history of Western thought because of the central role that he played in one of the most celebrated controversies that sprung up between the Order of Saint Dominic and the Society of Jesus. Both Dominicans and Jesuits based their arguments on the texts of Aquinas. The debate has come down to us as the *De Auxiliis* controversy, which eventually required the convocation of a papal commission or congregation of the same name in order to sort the issues out.[20] All in all, sixty-eight sessions were held between 1602 and 1605. The ecclesiastical authorities reached an irenic resolution, which received the endorsement of one of the great figures of the Catholic reform, Saint Francis de Sales (1567–1622). He became a saint but not especially a Thomist. As happens in many longstanding controversies, misunderstandings can arise. Sometimes Dominic Báñez appears in the secondary literature as an aberrant Thomist, as if he had lost his balance in the heat of debate. Báñez himself, on the other hand, professes otherwise: "Even in the least serious of questions, I never departed a hair's breadth from the doctrine of the Holy Doctor."[21] This star of the Thomist constellation died in 1604, before Pope Paul V expressed his wish on 5 September 1607 that both Dominicans and Jesuits "mutually abstain from harsh words expressing bitterness of spirit."[22]

It is noteworthy that the Thomist commentatorial tradition has successfully carried on the interpretation that Dominic Báñez rendered of Aquinas's teaching about grace and freedom.[23] This evolution should cause no surprise. Steven A. Long summarizes the basic philosophical doctrine at stake: "The effect of being is not properly contained by any created nature, either in essence or in operative power, and so, if the effect of being is to be achieved by a creature's operation, this requires that the creature be applied to action by divine power, moving it to

---

20. For a fair summary of the debate, especially the historical ins and outs, see R. J. Matava, *Divine Causality and Human Free Choice: Domingo Báñez, Physical Premotion and the Controversy* de Auxiliis *Revisited* (Leiden: Brill, 2016).
21. See his commentary on *Summa theologiae* 1a, q. 24, art. 6.
22. DS no. 1997.
23. The noted historian Pierre Mandonnet (d. 1936) explains Báñez's use of new language as required to distinguish Aquinas's thought from that of the new directions expressed by Molina and others. See Pierre Mandonnet, "Bañez, Dominique," in *Dictionnaire de Théologie Catholique* (Paris: Letouzey et Ané, 1932), 2.1: col. 145.

produce this effect."[24] No self-generated actors exist. What Aquinas says about how the gift of divine grace uplifts human actions to make them meritorious coheres with his general metaphysics of being and action. When this teaching is applied to the salvation of souls, Thomists hold with Aquinas that "predestination considered as an effect in its entirety has the divine goodness for its reason; to this the whole effect of predestination is ordered as to an end, and from this it issues as from its first moving principle."[25] They did not imagine, as Molina did, that predestination should be thought about in terms of two oarsmen, God and man, rowing the same boat.[26] Though the Báñezian account of divine grace coheres with Catholic teaching and Catholic practice, including sacramental practice, it still stokes fierce, though polite, contests among Catholic theologians.

Comprehensive Pedagogic and Apologetic Tools

By the start of the seventeenth century, many religious families other than Jesuits and Dominicans had taken up the teaching of Thomas Aquinas: Augustinians, Benedictines, Capuchins, Cistercians, Hieronymites, Mercedarians, Servites, and the Oratory, in the person of Blessed Juvenal Ancina (d. 1604). This development meant that the teaching of Aquinas would inform the education given to their new members. With this purpose in mind, the Discalced Carmelites in Spain set an example of pedagogical efficiency. The 1562 reform of the Carmelite Order that begins with Teresa of Ávila inaugurated a renewal of the intellectual life among the Discalced Carmelite friars. In 1613, these mendicant friars ordered the composition of manuals of philosophy and theology that would present Thomist doctrine in an organized manner. They relied on the texts of Aquinas but also on the sixteenth-century commentators, especially Cardinal Cajetan. The "Complutenses"—from the Latin name for the place where they worked, Alcalá de Henares—produced between 1624 and 1628 a four-volume set of Aristotelian-Thomist philosophy texts on natural philosophy and psychology. Although the course books were presented as a corporate work, individual friars produced the several volumes: Michael of the Holy Trinity (d. 1661), John of All Saints (d. 1654), and Anthony of the Mother of God (d. 1637). In 1640, a fifth volume on metaphysics

---

24. Long, "Providence," 559.
25. *Summa theologiae* 1a, q. 23, art. 5. Translation taken from Thomas Aquinas, *God's Will and Providence*, ed. and trans. Thomas Gilby, vol. 5 (1a. 19–26) of *Summa Theologiae* (London: Blackfriars, 1967), 127.
26. For the reference, see Cessario, "Molina and Aquinas," 308.

appeared by a French Discalced Carmelite. The manuals were written in a sophisticated though not esoteric style. The authors paid due attention to those of their contemporaries who took exception to elements of Aquinas's philosophical principles. It was held that no better defenders of Aquinas's philosophy could be found than among these Discalced Carmelites.[27] A definitive edition appeared in five quarto volumes at Lyons in 1670.

What the Complutenses did for Thomist philosophy, the Salmanticenses did for Thomist theology. From 1631, when the first treatises appeared at Salamanca, until 1883, when a revised edition in twenty volumes appeared at Paris, the twenty-four treatises on theological topics greatly influenced the shape and style of Catholic theology. The Carmelite theologians of Salamanca understood themselves to be commentators on the teaching of Aquinas. In fact, each disputation is identified with a specific text of the *Summa theologiae* (e.g., "On merit," *prima-secundae* q. 114). They also maintained a high level of metaphysical awareness. Theirs was a theology of the speculative variety that represents an eminent way of emphasizing the importance of Thomist principles. At the same time, these Carmelite theologians offer a good example of the elasticity of the Thomist commentatorial tradition. They follow Aquinas but arrive sometimes at specific conclusions that are proper to their own intellectual ethos. For example, they argue that the natural desire for God—a theme about which Thomists still debate—is natural in the sense that it appears *ut in pluribus* (frequently but not always) among the members of the human race.[28]

These Carmelite authors also show how the Thomist commentatorial tradition meshes with other religious strains of thought. Throughout the seventeenth and eighteenth centuries, Carmelites defended the spiritual teaching of both their master, Saint John of the Cross (d. 1591), and Saint Teresa of Ávila. One explicit testimony to this effort appears in a work by the Italian Carmelite author Baldassaro di S. Caterina di Siena (d. 1673), *Splendori riflessi di sapienza celeste*, published at Bologna in 1671. He allegorically represents the two saints as the two cherubim that Moses beholds when he enters the meeting tent and between whom God speaks to him (see Num 7:89). This comparison and the complete title, *Splendors of Heavenly Wisdom drawn from the Glorious Saints Thomas Aquinas and Teresa of Jesus*, give some hint of the devotion that surrounds the philosophical, speculative theological, moral theologi-

---

27. See Jean-Baptiste Gonet, *Clypeus Thomisticus*, Prologue.
28. See Salmanticenses, *Cursus theologicus*, tract. 2, disp. 1, dubium 3, §2, n. 40 (1:103–9).

cal, and mystical writings of the Discalced Carmelites.²⁹ In today's parlance, they clearly did theology on their knees.

Dominican Giants

The Portuguese-born Dominican John Poinsot (1589–1644) was the son of a Hapsburg government official. He did studies in Louvain, where he fell under the influence of a venerable Spanish teacher, Dominican Thomas de Torrès. In 1612, John himself made profession in the Dominican Order at Madrid. He adopted the title "of Saint Thomas." *Nomen est omen*. His previous studies enabled him soon to start lecturing at Alcalá de Henares where, according to the European system, he taught Dominicans at one of the university colleges, that of Saint Thomas. This seventeenth-century professor of theology, who began his teaching career at about the same time (ca. 1614) that the Mannerist painter El Greco died, would come to epitomize Spanish scholasticism at the end of the *siglo de oro*. John of St. Thomas rose in the university structure, first by obtaining the evening chair in theology and then the coveted morning chair, which was considered the prestigious time to lecture. All in all, John of St. Thomas spent thirty years giving university-level instruction in the doctrine of Saint Thomas Aquinas. In 1643, the Spanish king, Philip IV (d. 1665), who chose Diego Velázquez as court artist, also chose John as his confessor. The most important artist of the period worked side by side with the most important Thomist of the late Spanish Golden Age. Shortly thereafter, in 1644, while on a military campaign with the monarch, this grand master of the commentatorial tradition died of fever near Fraga in Aragon. Some allege that he was poisoned. About the same time and in the same place, Velázquez painted the king in the silver-and-rose costume he wore during the campaign.³⁰

Even in his own day, John of St. Thomas won recognition outside of the Dominican Order.³¹ The Iberian scholastic, though as mentioned above a near contemporary of Descartes, continues the lineage of the late medieval and renaissance commentators on Aquinas who chart a course different than that of "la pensée moderne."³² As Cajetan

---

29. Baldassaro di S. Caterina di Siena, *Splendori riflessi di sapienza celeste vibrati da gloriosi gerarchi Tommaso d'Aquino e di Teresa di Gesù* (Bologna, 1671).
30. The painting currently belongs to the Frick Collection in New York City. See Charles Ryskamp, Bernice Davidson, Susan Grace Galassi, Edgar Munhall, Nadia Tscherny, Richard Di Liberto, and Joseph Focarino, *Art in The Frick Collection: Paintings, Sculpture, Decorative Arts* (New York: Harry N. Abrams, 1996).
31. For example, see the plaudit in Salmanticenses, *Cursus theologicus, De spe*, disp. 4, dub. 4, n. 43.

opposed Scotus, and Báñez confronted Molina, so John defended a line of straight Thomist thought against the "eclecticism" of the Jesuit Francis Suárez (d. 1617).[33] The Dominican's prodigious literary output in both philosophy (e.g., *Cursus philosophicus Thomisticus* [1632–1636]) and theology (especially his *Cursus theologicus*, published in eight volumes starting in 1637) heavily influenced subsequent Thomist authors, including those of the twentieth century. John consciously appropriated the identity of a commentator. On his deathbed, he swore before the Blessed Sacrament that he never wrote anything that did not conform to the teaching of Thomas Aquinas.

Jacques Maritain, a discerning critic, considers John "one of the greatest metaphysicians in modern Western philosophy."[34] Indeed, recent students of John of St. Thomas's logic have uncovered therein a well-developed theory of semiotics.[35] Likewise, this master among Thomists remains a significant theological resource for contemporary theology, especially because of his treatment of the gifts of the Holy Spirit.[36] Beyond these recognitions, John of St. Thomas set down the charter for the Thomist commentatorial tradition in his 1637 *Tractatus de approbatione et auctoritate doctrinae d. Thomae*, a discussion of the authority that Saint Thomas enjoys in the church.[37] There we read that a true disciple of Aquinas—that is, a Thomist *tout court*—emerges as one who follows those who have already commented on Aquinas, who loves his teaching and seeks to defend and develop it, who shows sympathy for Aquinas's intuitions, who values his method of argument, and, in short, who holds fast to the commentatorial tradition. John of St. Thomas, who dies two hundred years after Capreolus, sets down criteria for identifying those authors, both his predecessors and his successors, who merit inclusion in the Thomist commentatorial tradition.

The heritage of Provençal Thomism that begins with John Capreolus

---

32. For an evaluation, see Cornelio Fabro, "Il posto di Giovanni di S. Tommaso nella Scuola Tomistica," *Angelicum* 66, no. 1 (1989): 56–90.
33. This important judgment is rendered by the celebrated twentieth-century Thomist, Santiago M. Ramirez in his article: "Jean de Saint-Thomas," in *Dictionnaire de Théologie Catholique* (Paris: Letouzey et Ané, 1947), vol. 8.1: col. 806.
34. See Jacques Maritain, "Address to the 4th Congress of the Portuguese World in July, 1940," in *Oeuvres complètes*, vol. 7, *1939-1943* (Paris: Éd. Saint-Paul, 1988), 1017–27.
35. For an interesting presentation of the *Ars logica*, first published at Alcalá de Henares in 1632, see *Tractatus de Signis: The Semiotic of John Poinsot*, arranged by John N. Deely, with Ralph Austin Powell (Berkeley: University of California Press, 1985).
36. For the text, see Joannes a Sancto Thoma, "De fructibus Spiritus Sancti," in *Cursus theologicus in summam theologicam d. Thomae*, q. 70, vol. 6 (Paris: Vivès, 1885). For example, see Javier Sese, "Juan de S.T. y su tratado de los dones del Espiritu Santo," *Angelicum* 66 (1989): 161–84. This issue of the journal commemorates the four hundredth anniversary of the birth of John of St. Thomas.
37. See John of St. Thomas, *Cursus theologicus* (Paris: Desclée et Socii, 1931) 1:221–301.

finds a seventeenth-century center in Toulouse, the city where Thomists flourished close to the tomb of their master. Among them, Vincent Contenson stands out as one notable variation on the Thomist pattern of pure speculative presentation that characterized many of his baroque contemporaries. Though he died early in life, Contenson managed to compose a multivolume work, *Theologia mentis et cordis seu speculationes universae doctrinae sacrae*, which saw several editions between 1668 and 1886. As the title, *A Theology of Mind and Heart*, suggests, he sought, in his own metaphor, to gather from the thorns of scholasticism the roses of piety.[38] The French Thomist theologians of the seventeenth century further confronted both the varieties of Jansenist claims and the ongoing disputes about predestination and moral theology. The work of Alexander Piny (d. 1709) *Quaestiones agitatae inter Thomistas et Molinistas*, published in 1666 at Lyons, reflects the temper of the times. These debated questions between Thomists and Molinists show that Catholic theologians of the period did not give up their microscopic examination of God's ways and man's lot.

John Baptist Gonet (d. 1681), another Toulouse Dominican, placed the whole of his theological compositions under the title of the *Clypeus theologiae thomisticae*, which was first published at Bordeaux between 1659 and 1669. Gonet resolutely mounted his "shield" of Thomistic theology—which provided a complete course in dogmatic theology—against its recent opponents. The book remained popular; a final edition appeared in Paris in 1876. Gonet's lifework finds its setting against the backdrop of the theoretical dramas that divided Latin Catholicism during the second half of the seventeenth century: Molinism, probabilism, and Jansenism. Despite his preferred pugilistic style, certain Thomists held Gonet suspect of sounding soft on Molinism. For their part, Molinists did not hesitate to allege that the Thomists were mere Jansenist clones. So much so, in fact, that Pope Benedict XIII, in 1727, felt obliged to pronounce that the teaching of Saint Thomas and the Thomist school had nothing to do with the errors of Cornelius Jansen (d. 1638).[39]

Gonet was not the only noteworthy Thomist to fall under suspicion of diluting the Thomist pure-predestination doctrine. The philosophical and theological treatises of the Paris Dominican Anthony Goudin

---

38. See Vincent Contenson, "Ad lectorem," in *Theologia mentis et cordis* (Cologne: 1722).
39. For the main points of Benedict XIII's bull *Pretiosus* (28 June 1727), see Heinrich Denzinger, *Compendium of Creeds, Definitions, and Declarations on Matters of Faith and Morals*, ed. Peter Hünermann, Robert Fastiggi, and Anne Nash, 43rd ed., Latin-English (San Francisco: Ignatius Press, 2012), no. 2509; and J. N. D. Kelly, *Oxford Dictionary of Popes* (New York: Oxford University Press, 1996), 293–95.

(d. 1695) fall on their own merits among the noteworthy contributions to the commentatorial tradition. Although Goudin defended Aquinas and the Thomist authors against eclectic interpretations of grace and freedom, he also may have looked for ways of establishing common ground, as it were, between Thomists and their main opponents. Unfortunately, his theological writings remained unpublished at his death, and certain Paris Dominicans did not consider it opportune to remedy the situation. Goudin, it was discovered, had enjoyed exchanges with Richard Simon (d. 1712), a controversial member of the French Oratory whose views on biblical criticism eventually ostracized him from mainstream Catholic life.

At the start of the new century, Louis XIV embarked on the War of Spanish Succession, a *guerre en dentelles*, which left a French nobleman, Philip, Duke of Anjou, on the throne of Spain. It was said that the Pyrenees disappeared. They did not. So, the brilliant age of Thomist commentators came to an end amidst unresolved controversies about Molinist views on human freedom, probabilist opinions about ethical conduct and the moral life, and Jansenist heterodoxies that distorted the way people understood the embrace of divine love. In addition to giving theoretical replies to these questions, Thomists also proffered practical solutions for living the gospel. The writings of the French diocesan priest Louis Mary Grignion de Montfort (d. 1716) display markedly Thomist characteristics. His *True Devotion to Mary* may be seen as a commentary on key features of Aquinas's teaching on the mediation exercised by Christ. Grignion de Montfort, who died a year after the French Sun King, Louis XIV, drew upon a work by the Jesuit theologian Jean Grasset, *La Véritable Dévotion envers la Sainte Vierge établie et défendue* (Paris, 1679). Grignion de Montfort shows that the Thomist pure-predestination doctrine occasions no cause for dread. He makes living Aquinas's teaching about salvation as easy as the saying of a single Ave Maria.[40]

Thomism flourished elsewhere than in the Franco-Iberian political arena. Benedict Ashley gives one example: "Seraphino Piccardi (d. 1695), noted for his excellent Latin style, taught at Padua and wrote ... a seven-volume defense of Thomism."[41] Above the Alps, the Benedictine university in Salzburg produced a number of "Salzburg Thomists,"

---

40. See Romanus Cessario, "Ave Maria! The Grace of Predestination," in *Thomism and Predestination: Principles and Disputations*, ed. Steven A. Long, Roger W. Nutt, and Thomas Joseph White (Ave Maria, FL: Sapientia Press, 2016), 226–38.
41. Benedict M. Ashley, *The Dominicans* (Collegeville, MN: Liturgical Press, 1990), 157.

including Ludwig Babenstuber (d. 1726). He defended the classical Báñezian views on *praemotio physica*, the phrase that captures the priority of the divine initiative in human willing and signals the Thomist preference for defending it.

8

Sentinels of Truth

The Supernatural under Attack

The well-known figures of the French Enlightenment, the *philosophes*, occupy the middle decades of the eighteenth century. Voltaire and Rousseau both die in 1778. In his book *La Crise de la conscience européenne*, the respected French cultural historian Paul Hazard observes aptly: "One day, the French people, almost to a man, were thinking like Bossuet. The day after, they were thinking like Voltaire. . . . It was a revolution."[1] At the same time, Enlightenment notions found their exponents in much of Europe and, under the influence of John Locke (d. 1704) and David Hume (d. 1776), also on the British Isles. This "Crisis of the European Mind," some opine, starts with Descartes, continues through the mechanistic world views of the seventeenth century, and issues in the Enlightenment proper.[2] Although the Enlightenment affected many different aspects of cultivated human life, Christian belief came under special attack. Reasonableness imposed its reductionist rule and measure on both theology and religious practice. In the widespread challenging of received

---

1. Paul Hazard, *The European Mind: The Critical Years (1680-1715)*, trans. J. Lewis May (New Haven: Yale University Press, 1953), xv.
2. See Jonathan I. Israel, *Radical Enlightenment: Philosophy and the Making of Modernity (1650-1750)* (Oxford: Oxford University Press, 2001), 14.

truths that emerged at the start of the eighteenth century, enlightened thinkers comfortably removed themselves from established forms of Christianity. Whereas in the sixteenth century, unbelief caused grave scandal, even among intellectuals, in the eighteenth century, this was not the case. Rousseau's popular "Profession of Faith of a Savoyard Vicar" replaced orthodox creedal Christianity with a form of unitarian universalism.[3] Other full-bodied attacks on the supernatural undermined revealed religion, its authorities (including the Bible), its institutions with their hierarchical structures, and its practices, especially the sacraments and devotions. In short, the perpetrators of reasonable, enlightened religion did everything in their power to ensure that their "religion" stood exempt from all impression of superstition. Superstition, it is said, moved Voltaire, famously, to cry out, "Ecrasez l'infâme!" (Crush the infamous thing).[4]

Thomists, with their inherited commitment to both faith and reason, stood up resolutely to the challenges of the Enlightenment. They did not succumb to rationalism; neither did they retreat into fideism. One clear example of a Catholic response to the Enlightenment assault on belief appears in the person of Vincent Louis Gotti (1664–1742), an Italian Dominican and later curial cardinal, who well represents how Thomists stood their ground before the challenges of enlightened thinkers. Noteworthily, he published in Rome a six-volume work, *Veritas religionis christianae*, between 1735 and 1740—years that also witnessed the composition of John Baptist Pergolesi's "Stabat Mater" (1736). As the subtitle of Gotti's tome makes plain, the *Truth of the Christian Religion* supplies a storehouse of user-friendly refutations against the arguments of "atheists, polytheists, idolaters, Muhammadans, and Jews." This well thought out apology for orthodoxy further bears witness to the power of the commentatorial tradition and its ability to sustain not only truth claims but also the theological life—that is, the life of Christian faith, hope, and charity—even in the face of fierce opposition and, indeed, ridicule. Gotti stood firm against the welter of putatively scientific and other claims that, according to secular intellectuals, impugned the credibility of Christian belief. With a confidence that arises only within someone who stands in sure possession of the principles of a divine science, Gotti countered the arguments made by such a key Enlightenment figure as Baruch Spinoza (d. 1677), a fore-

---

3. See Jean-Jacques Rousseau, *Emile, or On Education*, trans. Allan Bloom (New York: Basic Books, 1979), book 4, which contains the "Profession of Faith of the Savoyard Vicar."
4. See Guy Bedouelle, *The History of the Church* (London: Continuum, 2003), 126.

runner among those who popularized rationalist scriptural exegesis.⁵ In a word, Gotti insisted that Christian belief finds its legitimacy in the word of God, not in the hypotheses of scientific thinkers.

The curial cardinal was indeed an apologist for the Catholic religion *par excellence*. What is more important, Gotti accomplished his massive apologetic work after he had earlier published at Bologna, starting in 1727, his multivolume masterwork *Theologia scholastico-dogmatica juxta mentem d. Thomae Aquinatis ad usum discipulorum*.⁶ The phrase "according to the mind of Thomas Aquinas" indicates the author's intention to fulfill the description that John of St. Thomas set down as a criterion for one's being an authentic Thomist. At the same time, the qualification "for the use of his students" confirms that Gotti and Thomists in general exercised influence over a large number of educated Catholics. No ivory-tower theologians they; their print runs and editions show otherwise. Gotti rendered valuable services to the church, especially in Italy, where currents of thought from above the Alps influenced discussions conducted at the major centers of intellectual life. By the mid-eighteenth century, twenty-two universities served the Italian peninsula's major cities—Bologna being the oldest. Gotti also exemplifies the Thomist tradition practiced in service to the papacy. Although he studied at Salamanca, Gotti's career revolves around the Dominican priories in Bologna, which guard the relics of Saint Dominic, and at the Roman College of Saint Thomas, located until 1873 at the Minerva, where another Roman cardinal, Thomas de Vio, Cajetan, labored two centuries earlier. There in the church of Santa Maria sopra Minerva also repose the earthly remains of the Thomist poet Saint Catherine of Siena. Cardinal Gotti died in Rome on 18 February 1742.

Thomists Interpret Saint Thomas

Support for the school of Saint Thomas, as some refer to the commentatorial tradition, was not confined to Dominicans and other clerics. The Portuguese layman, Joseph Caetano (b. 1690), a professor of grammar in Lisbon, found occasion to take up a well-written defense of Aquinas. He responded to a dispute that involved the pastoral aspects of Aquinas's theological teaching. Under the influence of rigorist moral views about the sacrament of penance and reconciliation (commonly

---

5. Israel, *Radical Enlightenment*, 229, 455.
6. In English, this title runs: *Scholastic Dogmatic Theology According to the Mind of Saint Thomas Aquinas for Use by Students.*

called confession), some priest confessors in Portugal began the practice of requiring their penitents to reveal the names of their accomplices in sin, including sins of the flesh. These confessors became known as Anti-Sigillists, that is, they supposedly ignored the secrecy seal (*sigillum*) of the confessional. Some claimed that this aberrant practice found endorsement in the writings of Aquinas.[7] Caetano composed his *Escuela thomistica* to refute these claims.[8] The long Portuguese title of his "Letter" suggests the seriousness of purpose that motivated this devout, humanist scholar.[9] *Escuela thomistica* also indicates that the school of Saint Thomas flourished in Portugal. The University of Coimbra, founded in the late thirteenth century, long served as a center for the Thomist commentatorial tradition. Caetano, a Thomist of the eighteenth century, points to the enduring power of the Thomist school, even during a period of serious secularization, to maintain its sapiential poise. Although Coimbra, like other university centers, succumbed to the prevailing views of the eighteenth century, the faculty at Coimbra in the nineteenth century would move out from under the Enlightenment sky.

Thomists continued their lookout for probabilism and even opposed those moralists, such as Alphonsus Liguori (d. 1787), who argued for a moderate approach to this school of casuistry. For the Catholic believer who knows about the transformational power of divine grace, the seeking of expedient ways to escape challenging moral quandaries offers little attraction. Thomists further point out that sleek moral reasoning that ignores the truth about the good weakens the believer's reliance on the strong but sweet power of God's grace to overcome every obstacle. In other words, only the truth brings grace. Thomist moralists counsel the granting of forgiveness for sins, not the creating of excuses for them. Zeal for expressing moral truth occasionally can court misunderstanding. For example, John Vincent Patuzzi (1700–1769) developed a reputation for leaning toward rigorist views about moral conduct, even though he set forth his moral instruction with full attention paid to what the Scriptures and the tradition teach about the "new cre-

---

7. See Pierre-Curel Parisot, *Mémoires historiques sur les affaires des Jésuites avec le Saint Siège* (Lisbon: Ameno, 1766).
8. Joseph Caetano, *Escola Thomistica defendida das calumniosas injurias, con que os Antisigillistas a pretendiaõ affirmar patrocinadora de seus erros* (Lisbon: Sylviana, 1749).
9. The Lisbon earthquake of 1755 caused a setback to a Portuguese dictionary that Caetano had compiled. See Telmo Verdelho, "On the Origins of Modern Bilingual Lexicography: Interactions between Portuguese and Other European Languages," in *Perspectives on Lexicography in Italy and Europe*, ed. Silvia Bruti, Roberta Cella, and Marina Foschi Albert (Newcastle: Cambridge Scholars Publishing, 2009), 131n14.

ation" (see 2 Cor 5:17).[10] Patuzzi, however, was not a rigorist. For those who live in Christ as a new creation, right moral conduct may entail suffering, but it never lays "heavy burdens . . . on people's shoulders" (Matt 23:4). Patuzzi also defended Aquinas against injudicious critics who attributed to the Angelic Doctor views on the treatment of tyrants that, in fact, derive from other sources.[11] In other words, Patuzzi knew how to engage in a legitimate kind of source criticism.

In Spain, the Castilian moralist Vincent Ferrer Agramunt (1675–1738) upheld the moral vision of Aquinas against the overly legal focus on moral action that casuistry by its very nature generated. His two-volume summa of moral practice, published in Spanish at Valencia in 1736, was widely used throughout the Spanish-speaking world.[12] Earlier in France, Antoninus Massoulié (1632–1706) took up the battles that had engaged Thomist thinkers since the end of the sixteenth century. Since casuistry resulted in the severance of mystical theology from moral discourse, Massoulié composed particular explanations, in the form of meditations drawn from Aquinas's writings, of virtuous acts in conjunction with a discussion of the threefold division of the Christian life described as purgative, illuminative, and unitive.[13] He evidently considered these discussions pertinent to the execution of the moral life. In other words, this author wanted Catholics to learn how to concretize virtuous action and thereby discover personal solutions to moral dilemmas. Massoulié represents Thomists who recognize that standard Catholic casuistry relies too heavily on the lawyerly model for doing moral theology. In a casuist world, sinners pleaded the particulars of their moral dilemmas before a bar of legal experts who were known as approved authors in moral science. Thomists instead prefer to bring "the question about morally good action back to its religious foundations, to the acknowledgment of God, who alone is goodness, fullness of life, the final end of human activity, and perfect happiness."[14] The moral paradigm Aquinas sets down includes instruction

---

10. For example, his *Ethica christiana sive theologia moralis ex purioribus s. Scripturae divinaeque traditionis fontibus derivata, et s. Thomae Aquinatis doctrina continenter illustrata*, published between 1770 and 1790 in northern Italy.
11. For further discussion, see Thomas M. Osborne Jr., "*Dominium regale et politicum*: Sir John Fortescue's Response to the Problem of Tyranny as Presented by Thomas Aquinas and Ptolemy of Lucca," *Medieval Studies* 62, no. 1 (2000): 161–87.
12. Vincent Ferrer, *Summa moral para examen de curas y confesores* (Valencia, 1736).
13. In *Summa theologiae* 2a-2ae, q. 183, art. 4, Aquinas discusses three stages of Christian conversion—beginners, advanced, and perfect—whereas later theologians adopted the language of purgative, illuminative, and unitive.
14. *Veritatis Splendor*, no. 9. In Catholic thought, this 1993 Encyclical Letter of Pope John Paul II replaces casuist moral paradigms with a moral teleology.

about the vision of God as man's final happiness, the new life that sanctifying grace creates in the baptized, virtue's strengthening of the soul's operative capacities, and the special assistance that the gifts of the Holy Spirit bring by way of connaturality. In short, Thomists sought to develop well-tempered moral agents. To the extent that the virtuous person surrenders to the drawing power of the good, he or she does not require the assistance of a canon lawyer to discriminate between the permitted and the forbidden.

Antoninus Massoulié's moral writings appeared at Toulouse in the 1670s.[15] He later published his main work, a defense of the doctrine of physical premotion, at Rome.[16] Thomists never forget the lesson that Aquinas teaches by his ordering of materials in the *secunda pars* of the *Summa theologiae*. In a word, Aquinas places his treatment of the new law of grace and its transformational power before he begins to compose his detailed account of the virtues of the Christian life that makes up the *secunda-secundae*. So Thomists prefer to emphasize the priority of the divine initiative in human life before they begin to specify those rectified actions that lead to the possession of God's happiness. No surprise, then, to discover that Massoulié would confront the spurious claim advanced by some that Báñez invents *praemotio physica*. The teaching on physical premotion, Massoulié shows, originates with Aquinas himself and conforms to his overall teaching about the priority of the divine movement. To wit, God acts first in both the natural and graced movements of free creatures. In fact, Massoulié, in his address to his educated reader (*Erudito Lectori*), explains how the commentatorial tradition can remain true to itself: Thomists should remember that Aquinas serves as his own best interpreter. Even today, the best of the commentators observe this axiom, which separates them from eclectic and even putative Thomists.[17]

The commentatorial tradition received support from the various spiritual renewals that continued to invigorate Catholic life until the end of the eighteenth century. Much as the reform of Carmel in the sixteenth century led to the flourishing of Carmelite Thomist authors,

---

15. Antoninus Massoulié, *Méditations de S. Thomas sur les trois voies, purgatives, illuminative et unitive pour les exercises des dix jours* (Toulouse, 1678). For more about Toulouse dominating the region as a bastion of Catholic orthodoxy and reform, see Estelle Martinazzo, *Toulouse au Grand Siècle: Le rayonnement de la Réforme catholique (1590-1710)* (Rennes: Presses Universitaires de Rennes, 2015).
16. Antoninus Massoulié, *Divus Thomas sui interpres de divina motione et libertate creata* (Rome, 1692–1693).
17. Some authors continue to stress a distinction between the teaching of Aquinas and that of his commentators. As early as the seventeenth century, Antoninus Massoulié's work refuted—successfully in the view of many—a similar claim.

so also in France, starting with the Dominican reform of Sebastian Michaëlis (1543–1618), Thomist authors took inspiration from a renewed emphasis on the importance of the immaterial in human life. For vowed religious clerics, from whose ranks came the vast majority of eighteenth-century Thomist commentators, this meant living a sparse and observant life, that is, one shorn of unnecessary bourgeois excess. It bears remembering that the Provençal Dominican Sebastian Michaëlis counseled his followers to guard strictly the solitude of their conventual cells. Religious devotion further helps the theologian to remember that theology proceeds as a science of faith, a *fides quaerens intellectum*. Seventeenth-century theologians such as John Baptist Gonet; Vincent Baron (1604–1674), who strongly defended Aquinas's moral theology against both left-wing and right-wing critics; Vincent Contenson; Antoninus Reginald (1605–ca. 1676), known as the "Scourge" of Aquinas's adversaries; Anthony Goudin; and Antoninus Massoulié were formed in this observant school of Michaëlis. Baron especially displayed a sober resiliency in the face of polemical attacks from the probabilists.[18] All in all, the works of these Thomists show that religious devotion and intellectual discipline can produce the gold standard not only for Thomist commentators but also for Catholic theology. Such a high achievement finds its best home in a setting where study proceeds as a contemplative act. The lesson was not lost on those other Thomists who were not formally associated with a reform movement.

Models for Catholic Studies

On the banks of the Meuse sits the small commune of Revin, from whence emerges an important figure of the eighteenth-century Thomist commentatorial tradition, Charles René Billuart (1685–1757). A Dominican, Billuart spent his career in the cities of Liège, Douai, and in his hometown, where a Dominican priory stood under the patronage of the Veronese Dominican Saint Peter Martyr (d. 1252). Though located in France, in 1680 this priory came under the jurisdiction of the then newly established Dominican Province of Saint Rose in Flanders. There, at inconspicuous Revin, Billuart, whose compendia of theology were published into the twentieth century, was born and died.

---

18. For example, see Vincent Baron, *Sanctorum Augustini et Thomae vera et vna mens, de libertate humanâ, & gratiâ diuinâ, explicatur, & scholae thomisticae asseritur: aduersus duos Theophili Raynaudi libros, aliosque huius aetatis melioris notae theologos* (Paris: Simeonis Piget, 1666). Théophile Raynaud (d. 1663) was a Jesuit known for his polemical skills.

Billuart wins his place within the Thomist commentatorial tradition on account of his masterwork, *Summa S. Thomae hodiernis academiarum moribus acommodata*, first published at Liège between 1746 and 1751. A supplement to this monumental work was published posthumously in 1759. Throughout the second half of the eighteenth century and the nineteenth century, editions of Billuart's work appeared in Würzburg, Venice, Florence, Rome, Lyons, Arras, and Paris, where an edition at Vivès saw the light of day in 1890. Even so, Billuart recognized that his multivolume commentary on the *Summa* would not serve the needs of everyone. So he prepared an abridged edition, a *Summa Summae S. Thomae*, which appeared in many editions at different places between 1754 and 1903. Billuart's taking up of the Thomist commentatorial tradition received commendation from the Dominican authorities of his province. In fact, it was these superiors who asked Billuart to "accommodate" his speculative arguments to take account of the "contemporary" controversies in which Thomists engaged. In other words, the Flemish Dominicans had come to recognize that the Thomist commentatorial tradition was capable of meeting the theological and philosophical exigencies of a given period.

Billuart also showed himself to be a vigorous polemicist. In fact, Thomists stood in need of someone to answer their many critics. The papal bull *Unigenitus* (1713), issued by Pope Clement XI (d. 1721) and written into French law by 1730, brought about the practical end of Jansenism. However, both Jansenists and Molinists (for diverse reasons) argued that the papal bull also effected somehow a condemnation of the teachings of Saint Augustine and Saint Thomas on predestination and grace.[19] Billuart mounted a massive public relations campaign that sought to exculpate the Dominicans and other Thomists from the charge of adhering to Jansenist errors about grace and freedom. At the same time, he accomplished this task without capitulating to the modern infatuation with self-originating autonomy. Pierre Mandonnet lists some sixteen of Billuart's writings that reveal the tenor of the debates that Thomists undertook during the first half of the eighteenth century.[20] All in all, Billuart shows the vitality of the Thomist

---

19. For background to this controversy, see Sylvio Hermann De Franceschi, "Le Thomisme Moderne du Voisinage compromettant de l'Hérésie. L'École de saint Thomas entre calvinisme et jansénisme: parcours d'une inquiétude catholique au XVIIe siècle," in *Der Jansenismus—eine "katholische Häresie"?*, ed. Dominik Burkard and Tanja Thanner (Munster: Aschendorff Verlag, 2014), 163–92.
20. See Pierre Mandonnet, "Billuart, Charles-René" in *Dictionnaire de Théologie Catholique* (Paris: Letouzey et Ané, 1932), vol. 2.1: cols. 890–92.

commentatorial tradition that continued throughout the first six decades of the eighteenth century. His teaching and writings, his pulpit preaching, and his disputation with opponents, where he never lost the advantage, distinguish Billuart as an exemplary member of the Thomist school. And his peers recognized his achievements.[21]

At the height of the eighteenth century, Salvatore Roselli (1722–1784) represents a successful effort to continue Aquinas's philosophical thought. At the same time, his *Summa philosophica ad mentem angelici doctoris S. Thomae Aquinatis*, published at Rome between 1777 and 1783, adopted a new style of presentation.[22] Roselli distributed his philosophical arguments according to their disciplines: logic, physics, metaphysics, and ethics. Roselli also showed his appreciation for the earlier commentatorial tradition by making known again both the French Thomist J. B. Gonet and Noël (Natalis) Alexander (d. 1724), a seventeenth-century historian and polemicist whose dogmatic and moral theology Roselli published in an epitome, or abridged version. Because of his direct influence on later Thomists, Roselli stands out among the eighteenth-century carriers of the Thomist commentatorial tradition. After the political turmoil that disrupted Europe at the end of the century had subsided, Thomists turned to Roselli's *Summa philosophica* as a model for their philosophical instruction.[23] At the same time, this carrying on of the tradition occasioned some inconveniences. For example, Roselli, under the influence of common cultural axioms, specifically those of Gottfried Wilhelm Leibniz (d. 1716), introduced the principle of sufficient reason into Thomist philosophy. Later Thomists, however, corrected the distortion that this small brush with modern philosophy produced.[24] In retrospect, these twentieth-century authors again bear witness to the self-purifying capacities of the Thomist commentatorial tradition.

---

21. His epitaph commemorates his standing among his fellows: "Hic Jacet R. ac Eximius pater carolus-renatus billuart, Reviniensis, hujus conventus alumnus ac quinquies Prior, Collegii S. Thomae Duaci Regens, S. Theologiae Doctor, Necnon Provinciae Gallo-Belgicae ter Provincialis, vir scriptis et virtutibus clarus, religioni et orbi commendatissimus, Sed eheu! obiit 20 Januarii 1757, aetatis 73, Professionis 55, Sacerdotii 49. *Precare, moriture, ut requiescat in pace*" (A.F. Deodato Labye, "Vita Auctoris," in Charles René Billuart, *Summa S. Thomae hodiernis Academiarum moribus acommodata* [Lyon: Pelagaud et Lesne, 1839], 1: vii).
22. In English, *Philosophical Summa after the Mind of the Angelic Doctor*.
23. See Gerald A. McCool, *Nineteenth-Century Scholasticism: The Search for a Unitary Method* (New York: Fordham University Press, 1989), 85.
24. For example, see the discussion in H.-D. Gardeil, *Introduction to the Philosophy of St. Thomas Aquinas*, vol. 4, *Metaphysics*, trans. John A. Otto (St. Louis: Herder, 1967), 139–42.

Institutional Support

One eighteenth-century figure emerges as emblematic of the special care that the Dominican Order has given to the support of the Thomist commentatorial tradition. He is the redoubtable Spanish master of the Order John Thomas de Boxadors (1703–1780), whose life practically spans the peaceful moments of the century. He came to the Dominicans at an age later than was customary at the time. He was thirty and a lawyer by training. By 1756, the year that Handel produced his Italian-inspired opera "Atalanta" in London, Boxadors found himself at the helm of the Dominican Order, a post in which he remained until 1777. Although Boxadors produced none of the multivolume presentations of Thomist thought that the major Thomists of the modern period did, the Spanish master did support those who undertook this arduous work. The magnanimous publishing achievements of Salvatore Roselli, for instance, emerged as a result of the encouragement that Boxadors gave to his fellow Dominicans worldwide. His circular letter of 30 April 1757, "De renovanda et defendenda doctrina Sancti Thomae," explicitly encouraged a renewal of Thomist studies, that is, of both Thomas Aquinas and his commentators.

John Thomas Boxadors's plea for a renewal of the Thomist commentatorial tradition took place even as the effects of secularization began to weigh heavily on the clerics who were the carriers of the tradition. The Jesuits suffered under the secular resentment that, later, would adversely affect all religious clerics, including Benedictine monks, Dominican friars, and other religious priests. As early as 1759, a series of international intrigues gave cover to the Portuguese minister of state, the infamous Marquis of Pombal (d. 1782), to initiate the suppression of the Jesuits. Since the Portuguese Empire, Portuguese Overseas, was the first global empire in history, this policy also affected Catholic institutions from East Timor and Macao to Angola and Brazil. In 1773, after a series of suppressions in other European countries, Pope Clement XIV (d. 1774), a former Franciscan, suppressed the Jesuits worldwide, although in the Russian Empire Catherine the Great (d. 1796) ignored the pope and welcomed exiled Jesuits. Without their institutions, the Jesuits' dissemination of Aquinas's text suffered grave, though not, as later events prove, absolute, impediment. Another indication of the religious temper of the times comes from the premiere in 1786 of Mozart's *The Marriage of Figaro*. The eighteenth century witnesses the apogee of comic opera, the *opera buffa*. One may surmise, however, that neither Thomist metaphysics nor casuist moralism weighed heavily on the superficial minds of those who frequented these frothy divertissements.

Boxadors was not to become the last hurrah. Until they became impeded by political repression, Dominicans and others continued to devote themselves to the teaching of Aquinas. Throughout the eighteenth century, Thomists carried on the commentatorial tradition. Besides Portugal, Spain, France, Belgium, and Italy, they also saw their tomes published in Bohemia, Poland, Germany, and Holland. English-speaking Thomists from the British Isles who had established themselves on the Continent published their works mainly at Louvain, especially at the start of the eighteenth century. At least nine commentaries on Aquinas by eighteenth-century Dominicans and other authors saw the light of day in the New World, including one printed in the Spanish colonial city of Puebla and three in Colombia.[25] In Europe, other religious clerics augmented the numbers of Thomist teachers and writers. These included members of Catholic religious orders such as the Augustinians, Benedictines, Cistercians, Minims, and the Vincentian or Lazarist fathers who taught at Piacenza in Italy. Thomist authors even published in Armenia and Russia.

Boxadors's enthusiasm for Thomist theologians reached Europe's crowned heads. In 1760, the empress Maria Theresia (d. 1780) called the Italian Dominican Peter Mary Gazzaniga (1722–1799) to Vienna for service in public instruction. He lectured there on theology to audiences graced by the presence of eminent personages not excluding Pope Pius VI (when he came to the capital city in 1782). And although her successor, Joseph II (d. 1790), ceded little to the pope, the enlightened monarch did grant Gazzaniga a yearly pension of three hundred florins. The lectures that Gazzaniga delivered at the University of Vienna were published in Bologna in nine volumes between 1788 and 1793. Many other editions of his *Praelectiones theologicae habitae in Vindobonensi Universitate* followed. This author taught straight Thomist doctrine, especially about controversial issues such as predestination and human freedom. He took seriously the instruction that Pope Benedict XIII had given to his fellow Dominicans in 1724, which, in a word, counseled them to stand fast despite the misunderstandings that oth-

---

25. See Leonard A. Kennedy, *A Catalogue of Thomists, 1270–1900* (Houston: Center for Thomistic Studies, 1987), 133–53. Anthony de Torres (*De Gloriosissimo Ecclesiae doctore* [Angelopoli, 1695]) illustrates early Mexican Thomist thought.

ers generated about their authentic interpretation of Thomas Aquinas.[26]

Survival

When rebel soldiers captured the French king and his immediate family at Varennes in June 1791, French revolutionary spirit reached a turning point that culminated with the execution of Louis XVI on 21 January 1793. With the fall of the monarchy, the French Revolution turned against Catholicism. By the end of the infamous year, every Dominican convent in France had been suppressed by the French revolutionary regime. Gone were the thirteenth-century royal archers who protected Aquinas in the City of Lights. Not everyone in France, however, welcomed the revolution. One contemporary critic, Louis Gabriel Ambroise, vicomte de Bonald (d. 1840), observed that once French "manners were lighthearted and our minds were serious. The Revolution changed all that," he wrote, "It made our minds superficial and our manners grave. Today we have neither reason nor joy."[27] In France, things did not start to change for the better until, in 1839, Henri-Dominique Lacordaire (d. 1861) issued his *Mémoire pour le rétablissement en France des Frères Prêcheurs*, a plea to restore religious life in France.[28] By that time, the Napoleonic era and its political reforms had run their course throughout Europe. The Congress of Vienna (1815) restored a certain civility to a Europe that had undergone nearly twenty-five years of revolutionary turmoil and ideologically ridden reforms.

Between 1801 and 1814, Napoleon sought to impose his rule of cultural conformity on the religious practices of northern Italy. One author dubs his effort the "the war against God."[29] The exile of foreign clerics from cities to which they had come by invitation of a well-meaning prince—for example, the Dominicans at Piacenza—offers a glimpse of the disturbances that imperial expansion caused to the set-

---

26. For more discussion of Pope Benedict XIII's support of the Thomists, see Sylvio Hermann De Franceschi, *La Puissance et la Gloire. L'orthodoxie thomiste au péril du jansénisme (1663-1724): le zénith français de la querelle de la grâce* (Paris: Nolin, 2011).
27. Louis Gabriel Ambroise de Bonald, *Pensées sur divers sujets, et discours politiques*, in *Critics of the Enlightenment: Readings in the French Counter-Revolutionary Tradition*, ed. and trans. Christopher Olaf Blum (Wilmington, DE: ISI Books, 2004), 74.
28. For further information, see André Duval, "La curie romaine devant le projet Dominicain de Lacordaire 1838-1839," in *Lacordaire: son pays, ses amis et la liberté des ordres religieux en France*, ed. Guy Bedouelle (Paris: Les Éditions du Cerf, 1991), 91-109. This volume also contains information on the restoration of other religious clerics in France. Several of these groups would contribute to the later Thomist commentatorial tradition.
29. For a detailed discussion, see Michael Broers, *The Politics of Religion in Napoleonic Italy: The War against God, 1801-1814* (London: Routledge, 2002).

tled routines of Italian life.³⁰ At the same time, study and learning continued under the auspices of the dioceses. Vincent Benedict Buzzetti (1777–1824) was born at Piacenza. As a youth, he studied at the Vincentian (Lazarist) Alberoni College.³¹ The Masdeu brothers, Spanish ex-Jesuits who were Suarezian Thomists passing their exile in Italy, gave lessons to Buzzetti in philosophy and theology at the former Jesuit College of Saint Peter until 1806 when the French occupiers shut it down.³² Thereafter, except for the time required to obtain his doctorate at the Roman Sapientia, Buzzetti taught at the diocesan seminary in Piacenza until his death. As a mark of recognition, he was named a "theological" canon of the Piacenza cathedral.

Dissatisfied with the empiricist philosophical outlooks that followed upon John Locke and, even more, Étienne Bonnot de Condillac (d. 1780), Buzzetti looked for an alternative to hardcore empiricism. While still a student at the Alberoni College, he discovered the Thomist philosophical manual of Salvatore Roselli, which taught him about the real distinction between essence and existence. Additionally, the Thomist teaching on grace, mediated by the writings of Cardinal Cajetan and John of St. Thomas, gave Buzzetti a different perspective on the movement of divine grace than what his earlier, former-Jesuit teachers, who represented late-scholastic Molinism, had given him. Canon Buzzetti turned to Thomist thought because he found that the popularized philosophical outlooks of the Enlightenment did not favor Catholic truth. He also practiced the commentatorial tradition at a time when political realities made it difficult for the church to carry on its teaching mission. His legacy survives, at least partially, on account of two students he taught in the diocesan seminary, the Sordi brothers, Dominic and Serafino. As Leonard Boyle recounts it: "When the Jesuit Order, suppressed since 1773, was restored by Pius VII in 1814, these two Sordi brothers joined it, bringing with them some of Buzzetti's enthusiasm for Thomas."³³ The Thomist commentatorial tradition and the writings of the saint who inspires it survived the destructive regimes that, for a time, asserted themselves in France, Spain, and Austria as well as on the Italian peninsula, even in the Papal States. This outcome causes no surprise to the Thomist who realizes that the

---

30. Ibid., 119–21.
31. The college bears the name of its founder, Cardinal Giulio Alberoni (1664–1752), a controversial ecclesiastic who turned a leprosarium into a seminary for priesthood candidates.
32. Washington's Georgetown University, founded in 1789, suffered no such blow.
33. Leonard E. Boyle, "A Remembrance of Pope Leo XIII: The Encyclical *Aeterni Patris*," in *One Hundred Years of Thomism*, ed. Victor B. Brezik (Houston: Center for Thomistic Studies, 1981), 16.

contingencies of history do not escape "the unchangeable and certain order of divine Providence."[34]

---

34. *Summa theologiae* 1a, q. 23, art. 4, ad 2.

9

Sound Philosophy for Catholic Doctrine

A Providential Awakening

Throughout the nineteenth and early twentieth centuries, the influence of modern philosophy on Catholic theologians did not always result in their generating a clear exposition of Catholic truth. Even good-intentioned efforts to defend the tenets of the Catholic religion erred by their overreliance on popular philosophical idiom. In a lecture that he delivered at Mount Saint Bernard Seminary in 1962 in Dubuque, Iowa, the eminent James A. Weisheipl observed that during "the eighteenth and nineteenth century countless Catholic textbooks were produced which presented a 'Christian philosophy' based on the Scriptures, Descartes, Newton and [Christian] Wolf."[1] Admittedly, the authors of these textbooks sought to produce a Catholic apologetic for the supernatural mysteries that the church taught and practiced. Unfortunately, however, their efforts fell short of the mark. "Their Wolffian epistemology," one writer explains, "undermined the coherence of their philosophy. Their deductive notion of science, based on intuitive first principles and modeled upon the Cartesian ideal of necessary certitude and apodictic evidence, was no longer the notion of science upon which St. Thomas had molded his speculative theology."[2]

---

1. James A. Weisheipl, "The Revival of Thomism as a Christian Philosophy," in *New Themes in Christian Philosophy*, ed. Ralph M. McInerny (Notre Dame: University of Notre Dame Press, 1968), 167.

Reaction appeared in the writings of two prominent figures of nineteenth-century Catholic intellectual life. George Hermes (d. 1831) and Anton Günther (d. 1863) developed, respectively, a Christian Kantianism and a Christian Hegelianism that purported to supply rational arguments for those mysteries to which unaided reason, so the church insists, cannot attain. In other words, they attempted to move beyond devising philosophical pointers to the supernatural and aimed instead at mounting philosophical proofs for the revealed truths that only divine and Catholic faith can make known. In a brief on 26 September 1835, Pope Gregory XVI denounced Hermes posthumously for teaching that "reason is the chief norm and only medium whereby man can acquire knowledge of supernatural truths."[3] Later, Pope Pius IX, in his brief on 15 June 1857, condemned Günther's influential books for making human reason and philosophy a "master" over supernatural faith.[4] The papal admonitions plugged holes in the dike, as it were, but they did not provide a corrective to the intellectual vacuum that had developed in the wake of the political upheavals that followed upon the French Revolution. The sad ending of Félicité Robert de Lamennais (d. 1854), who though once a brilliant apologist for Catholic doctrine died alienated from the church, provides one example of the waywardness a fatherless generation of Catholic thinkers can create.

The general religious and theological turmoil that characterized early nineteenth-century Catholic life impeded but did not destroy the Thomist commentatorial tradition. The impetus given to the Dominicans by John Thomas de Boxadors ensured that the teaching of the Angelic Doctor remained normative throughout the Order to which Aquinas belonged.[5] At the same time, the restoration of the Jesuits in 1814 gave institutional support to those, such as the Sordi brothers, who had developed an appreciation for the thought of Aquinas when they were students of Canon Vincent Buzzetti. Both Sordis entered the Society of Jesus. Serafino Sordi (d. 1865) taught in various Italian set-

---

2. Gerald A. McCool, *Nineteenth-Century Scholasticism: The Search for a Unitary Method* (New York: Fordham University Press, 1989), 29. Father McCool's account of the period considers the significant Thomist figures, especially the Jesuits at the Gregorianum, in relation to later twentieth-century views adopted by Catholic theologians.
3. Heinrich Denzinger, *Compendium of Creeds, Definitions, and Declarations on Matters of Faith and Morals*, ed. Peter Hünermann, Robert Fastiggi, and Anne Nash, 43rd ed., Latin-English (San Francisco: Ignatius Press, 2012), no. 2738.
4. Ibid., no. 2829.
5. The Dominican General Chapter held in Rome in 1838 invoked Boxadors's circular letter of 1757 that promoted the study of Aquinas. See Leonard E. Boyle, "A Remembrance of Pope Leo XIII: The Encyclical *Aeterni Patris*," in *One Hundred Years of Thomism*, ed. Victor B. Brezik (Houston: Center for Thomistic Studies, 1981), 14–15.

tings, including Modena, where in the early 1830s he became friends with a Jesuit confrere, Joseph Pecci, the brother of the future Pope Leo XIII. Serafino's older brother, Dominic Sordi (d. 1880), generated interest among a group of students in a scholastic revival that won the support of the Jesuit Provincial in Naples, Louis Taparelli D'Azeglio (1793–1862), brother of the noteworthy Italian politician Massimo D'Azeglio. Taparelli's Jesuit superiors, however, disbanded the group of incipient Thomists that he and Sordi sustained within the Jesuit scholasticate at Naples. Both Jesuits were assigned elsewhere. Fortunately, however, the Jesuit sent to replace Dominic Sordi, who was considered to be the revolutionary group leader, himself became convinced of the Thomist cause. Jesuit Father Matthew Liberatore (1810–1892) served the church well both as a teacher and as a counselor to the Holy See. In this capacity, he helped frame the responses to the abovementioned heterodoxies spawned by both Hermes and Günther. As Father Liberatore's obituary notes: after his return to Naples—having taken refuge in Malta from the revolutionary political movements of 1848—Liberatore "taught theology, and it was then that he fully realized the danger to which the prevailing systems of philosophy were exposing the theological student by the decided and steady departure which manifested itself, from the methods of the scholastic system as formulated by the Angelic Doctor."[6] The Kingdom of the Two Sicilies, a prosperous political entity under the Spanish Bourbons, supplied (at least until 1861 when the last monarch, Francis II, ceded to the forces of Italian unification) a seedbed for a rejuvenation of interest in the texts and thought of Saint Thomas Aquinas whose own life is associated so dearly with this city.

One of the fruits of the incipient renewal of interest in Aquinas that circulated within cosmopolitan Naples appears in the figure of a diocesan priest named Cajetan Sanseverino (d. 1865). At first, he followed the popular Christian Cartesian apologists that both Hermes and Günther had found unconvincing. Providence intervened, however, and Sanseverino was saved from following their errors. Instead, the philosophical manual of the Thomist Salvatore Roselli, and perhaps personal contact with the suspect Dominic Sordi, moved Sanseverino to realize that the restoration of philosophy required resources that were composed before the seventeenth century. By 1853, Sanseverino punctured the myth that accommodation to whatsoever prevailing philo-

---

6. For an American appreciation, see "P. Matteo Liberatore, S.J.," *American Ecclesiastical Review* 7, no. 6 (1892): 441–45.

sophical paradigm, no matter its provenance or prominence, establishes the benchmark for doing Catholic theology. Sanseverino produced a five-volume *Philosophia Christiana*, published in Naples in 1853. One of his disciples, another diocesan priest, Nunzio Signoriello (d. 1889), published in 1894 his own *Compendio della filosofia christiana* as well as a lexicon that helped students become familiar with the philosophical vocabulary of Aquinas. Signoriello represents the hundreds of philosophical textbooks published during the second half of the nineteenth century by Dominicans, Jesuits, members of other religious orders (especially the Vincentian Fathers at Piacenza), diocesan priests, and other educators in Italy. The works of Saint Thomas began to be published in Bourbon Naples as early as 1845. In fact during the first half of the nineteenth century, Naples afforded a more favorable environment for the study of Aquinas than did Rome. One Jesuit author explains this circumstance by the fact "that a Thomistic tradition still existed among the Neapolitan Dominicans."[7] In any case, the Neapolitan Thomists clearly took their charge seriously. Attention to the texts of Aquinas remains a hallmark of the authentic commentatorial tradition, even when it happens that the commentators themselves employ words or phrases that represent the thought, though perhaps not the exact terminology, of Aquinas.

Roman Revival

The Dominican convent at the Minerva suffered expropriation in 1873 at the hands of the newly unified Italian government. This unfortunate turn of events, however, did not inhibit the remarkable zeal of Francis Zigliara (1833–1893), whose religious name in the Dominican Order was Thomas Mary. This young Dominican, after having been sent to Perugia for his theological studies, received priestly ordination at the hands of the then-archbishop and later pope, Joachim Pecci. The best testimony to the esteem in which Pope Leo XIII held this Dominican appeared when Zigliara received the red hat of a cardinal at the first consistory that Pope Leo held after his election in 1879. What is more important, Cardinal Zigliara enjoyed a reputation for brilliance. His lectures at the College of Saint Thomas, which survived the loss of its historical location near the tombs of both Catherine of Siena and Cardinal Cajetan, drew students from around Rome. Legend has it that the pope himself secretly—that is, seated veiled behind a white curtain—would join

---

7. McCool, *Nineteenth-Century Scholasticism*, 85.

those who listened to Zigliara expound the principles of Saint Thomas's thought.[8] Like so many Thomists of the Leonine period, Zigliara published his course lectures. His *Summa philosophica* appeared in 1887 both at Lyons and Paris.

Outside of Italy, Ceferino González y Díaz Tuñón (1831–1894), also a Dominican, represents the accomplishments of Thomists in Spain and the Spanish colonies of the New World. Before he was called to serve the Spanish hierarchy and subsequently made a residential cardinal in 1884 by Pope Leo XIII, González proved himself knowledgeable in divers religious, philosophical, scientific, and social sciences.[9] Although González never worked in Rome, his devotion to Thomism solidified the movement that Pope Leo XIII was bent on promoting and that achieved a certain apex in the 1879 publication of the encyclical *Aeterni Patris*. The Jesuit priest Joseph Kleutgen (1811–1883), a Westphalian by birth, ranks alongside the two Dominicans as representative figures of Thomism during the period of Pope Leo XIII's pontificate. This learned Jesuit often falls among those who are said to have contributed to the drafting of Leo's famous encyclical. Kleutgen, however, earned his reputation as a critic of Hermes and Günther, such that Pope Leo XIII, upon hearing of Kleutgen's death, pronounced him worthy of the appellation "Prince of the Philosophers."

Pope Leo XIII merits high praise for his encyclical *Aeterni Patris*, whose subject matter the pope himself describes as "on the restoration in Catholic schools of Christian philosophy according to the mind of the Angelic Doctor Saint Thomas Aquinas." The text was promulgated on 4 August 1879, then the liturgical feast of Saint Dominic, founder of the Dominicans. In 1998, more than a century after the publication of *Aeterni Patris*, Pope John Paul II gave what may be considered an official account of what his predecessor, Pope Leo XIII, had accomplished.

> The positive results of the papal summons are well known. Studies of the thought of Saint Thomas and other Scholastic writers received new impetus. Historical studies flourished, resulting in a rediscovery of the riches of Medieval thought, which until then had been largely unknown; and there emerged new Thomistic schools. With the use of historical method, knowledge of the works of Saint Thomas increased greatly, and many scholars had courage enough to introduce the Thomistic tradition into the philosophical and theological discussions of the day. The most influ-

---

8. Boyle, "Remembrance," 21.
9. For a sampling, see his *Estudios religiosos, filosóficos, científicos y sociales* (Madrid: Policarpo López, 1873).

ential Catholic theologians of the present century, to whose thinking and research the Second Vatican Council was much indebted, were products of this revival of Thomistic philosophy. Throughout the twentieth century, the Church has been served by a powerful array of thinkers formed in the school of the Angelic Doctor.[10]

In this 1998 authoritative text, the pope also acknowledged that during the time since 1879, the church likewise benefited from other philosophical initiatives, though he does not identify them. Pope John Paul II does, however, indicate the criterion by which one should judge non-Thomist proposals: "From different quarters, modes of philosophical speculation have continued to emerge and have sought to keep alive the great tradition of Christian thought which unites faith and reason."[11] This acknowledgment of diverse intellectual movements within Catholic thought should not, however, leave the impression that *Aeterni Patris* fell short of making a profound impact on the continuance of the Thomist commentatorial tradition. Throughout the twentieth century, Papal magisterial documents cited the texts of Aquinas. Pope John Paul II acknowledged, in fact, that "the Church has been justified in consistently proposing St. Thomas as a master of thought and a model of the right way to do theology."[12]

After *Aeterni Patris*

One fine exemplification of the usefulness that Aquinas serves for explaining Catholic teaching appears in the person of the pope who signed the encyclical. Pope Leo XIII wrote important encyclicals on a wide range of matters that perennially concern the church of Christ: social problems, government, human liberty, Catholic action, and education. Perhaps the best known encyclical, judged by the celebration of its publication by succeeding Roman Pontiffs, remains the encyclical on capital and labor, *Rerum novarum* (revolutionary changes).[13] More directly related to the development of the Thomist commentatorial tradition, historians of the period note that after *Aeterni Patris*, "outstanding Catholic scholars directed their ability to promulgating the

---

10. *Fides et ratio*, no. 58.
11. Ibid., no. 59.
12. Ibid., no. 43.
13. See Pope John Paul II, Encyclical Letter, *Centesimus annus*, no. 5: "The 'new things' to which the Pope devoted his attention were anything but positive. The first paragraph of the Encyclical describes in strong terms the 'new things' (*rerum novarum*) which gave it its name: 'That the spirit of revolutionary change which has long been disturbing the nations of the world.'"

philosophy and theology of the Angelic Doctor."[14] During the remaining twenty years of the nineteenth century, hundreds of Thomist studies were produced by authors all over the world. Furthermore, in the wake of *Aeterni Patris*, publishers supplied editions of the works of Saint Thomas, both in Latin and in translation. Pope Leo, aided by his confidant, Cardinal Zigliara, set up a commission (still functioning as the Leonine Commission) in order to ensure the publication of a critical edition of Aquinas's *opera omnia*. The nine volumes of the *Summa theologiae*, annotated by Cardinal Cajetan's sixteenth-century commentary, were published between 1888 and 1906.[15]

Aeterni Patris affected the institutional life of the church. Catholic intellectuals met in congresses.[16] Learned journals dedicated to Thomist studies like the *Revue Thomiste* began to appear.[17] Organizations to promote the teaching and the thought of Saint Thomas Aquinas received recognition. Foremost among them remains the Pontifical Academy of Saint Thomas Aquinas, which was founded on 15 October 1879 by Pope Leo XIII himself. The pope confided the presidency of this academy to his brother, Cardinal Joseph Pecci, a Jesuit, and also to the Dominican Thomas Zigliara. Other institutes appeared in Italy, France, Belgium, Germany, and Fribourg in Switzerland. In the United States, the American Dominicans, who had operated a general *studium* (study house) in Ohio since 1834, made the decision in 1902 to move to Washington, DC, where the Dominican House of Studies remains a vital center of intellectual life.[18] All in all, the ripple effect throughout the Catholic world that *Aeterni Patris* generated reveals an enormous intellectual achievement. Sometimes, authors refer to the period after *Aeterni Patris* as Leonine Thomism or even Neo-Thomism. However, as the preceding chapters have indicated, the periodization of the Thomist commentatorial tradition can suggest wrongly that the thought of Aquinas has only enjoyed intermittent popularity. In fact, as has been put forward in this book, Aquinas and his commentators lay

---

14. Weisheipl, "Revival of Thomism," 177.
15. For more information, see Jean-Pierre Torrell, *Aquinas's Summa: Background, Structure, and Reception* (Washington, DC: Catholic University of America Press, 2005), 108–16.
16. Guy Bedouelle (*The History of the Church* [London: Continuum, 2003], 146) points out that these exercises were "soon to be interrupted by the modernist crisis."
17. See Henry Donneaud, "Grandeurs et limites d'un projet thomiste dominicain sous les pontificats de Léon XIII et Pie X: Les premières années de la *Revue thomiste*," in *La Province dominicaine de Toulouse (XIXe-XXe): Une histoire intellectuelle et spirituelle*, Henry Donneaud, Augustin Laffay, and Bernard Montagnes (Paris: Éditions Karthala, 2015), 137–49.
18. For more information, see J. A. Di Noia, "*Discere et Docere*: The Identity and Mission of the Dominican House of Studies in the Twenty-First Century," *The Thomist* 73, no. 1 (2009): 111–27.

claim to a continuity that dates back at least to his canonization at the start of the fourteenth century, and even earlier.

One indication of the perennial vitality that Thomist thought enjoys appears in its demonstrated capacity to capture the minds of some of the most intelligent spirits of an age. Their embrace of Aquinas oftentimes accompanies a discovery of the Catholic Church. Of the many examples that may be named, Jacques Maritain (1882–1973) and his wife, Raïssa (d. 1960), come to mind. They made significant contributions to sustaining the Thomist commentatorial tradition once they were baptized in 1906, a year after they had met Léon Bloy (d. 1917), of whom Raïssa Maritain said, "You have done everything for me, since you brought me to know God."[19]

Other Thomists of the early twentieth century escaped the fatuity of claims advanced by secular learning. Foremost among them stands the figure of a French Thomist, Father Reginald Garrigou-Lagrange (1877–1964).[20] He was born at Auch in the Gascon region of France. Once ordained a priest in the Dominican Order, his work in France at the Paris *studium* Le Saulchoir was brief. In 1909, he was called to Rome to begin a teaching career at the Pontifical University of Saint Thomas Aquinas, the Angelicum and successor to the College of Saint Thomas at the Minerva. Except during the summer vacation periods when he gave retreats and conferences, mainly in French-speaking sections of Europe, Garrigou-Lagrange spent his long career of service to the church entirely in Rome where, after patiently enduring a long and distressing illness, he died on 15 February 1964. In addition to his much-appreciated teaching and copious writing, the French Dominican served as an advisor to several important Roman Congregations. An obituary in the French secular press reported that Father Garrigou-Lagrange shone with a certain presence, for he was both a theologian and a truly spiritual man, one who taught more by his personal witness than by his words.[21]

Like his Thomist predecessors of the nineteenth century, Garrigou-Lagrange tackled the problems that the moderns raised against the Catholic religion. In order to better demonstrate the thoroughly distinctive and utterly gratuitous quality of Christian revelation, Gar-

---

19. Jacques Maritain, "In Homage to our Dear Godfather Leon Bloy," in *Untrammeled Approaches*, trans. Bernard Doering (Notre Dame: University of Notre Dame Press, 1997), 34.
20. For a complete bibliography of Father Garrigou-Lagrange's works, see B. Zorcolo, "Bibliografia del P. Garrigou-Lagrange," *Angelicum* 42 (1965): 200–272.
21. For further information, see Romanus Cessario, "Garrigou-Lagrange, Reginald," in *Dizionario di Mistica*, ed. Luigi Borriello et al. (Città del Vaticano: Libreria Editrice Vaticana, 1998).

rigou-Lagrange articulated a finely structured rational apologetic. His *De Revelatione per Ecclesiam catholicam proposita* affirms that God chooses to communicate what he alone knows about himself, so that intelligent creatures can come to an authentic knowledge of those things that surpass the grasp of human understanding.[22] Theological faith, asserts Garrigou-Lagrange (following Aquinas), represents an essentially supernatural gift by which the human person comes to assent to divine truths. While Father Garrigou-Lagrange defended the objective value and immutability of the teaching of faith, he was at the same time fully aware of the *via negativa*. For example, in *Le sens du mystère et le clair obscure intellectuel*, Garrigou-Lagrange expressly teaches that between the Creator and the creature, one never finds a similitude that is not accompanied by an even greater dissimilitude.[23] In other words, Garrigou-Lagrange was no rationalist. He was, however, an eminent exponent of realism, as one of his first publications, *Le sens commun*, and his masterful *La synthèse thomiste*, translated immediately in 1950 into English with the title *Reality*, make plainly evident.[24]

The temptation exists to consider Garrigou-Lagrange the final flowering of the Thomist renewal that Leo XIII initiated in 1879. This Dominican Thomist died in 1964 as the Second Vatican Council (1962–1965) was in session. Some view this council as marking a break with the theological styles that Garrigou-Lagrange so well represents. From hindsight of more than a half century, the fact remains that the distinguished Thomist and his works enjoy a popularity that testifies to the enduring originality of Aquinas's thought. Those who would practice the commentatorial tradition in the twenty-first century cannot proceed without acquainting themselves with the main works of Father Garrigou-Lagrange.[25] Is it too much to think that his student Karol Wojtyła had his teacher in mind when later, as pope, he penned these prescient words about faith and reason?

---

22. The first edition was published in 1918 by Gabala in Rome, Paris, and Ferrara; other editions followed in 1931 and 1945. For an English version, see T. J. Walshe, *The Principles of Catholic Apologetics; A Study of Modernism Based Chiefly on the Lectures of Pere Garrigou-Lagrange "De Revelatione per Ecclesiam Catholicam proposita," adapted and rearranged* (London: Sands, 1926).
23. This book was first published by Descleé de Brouwer at Paris in 1934 and translated into other languages but not English.
24. *Le sens commun; la philosophie de l'être et les formules dogmatiques. Suivi d'une étude sur la Valeur de la critique moderniste des preuves thomistes de l'existence de Dieu* (Paris: Beauchesne, 1909); and *La synthèse thomiste* (Paris: Brouwer, 1950). The latter volume was translated into English under the title *Reality: A Synthesis of Thomistic Thought*, trans. Patrick Cummins (St. Louis: Herder, 1950).
25. For example, see the study by Aidan Nichols, *Reason with Piety: Garrigou-Lagrange in the Service of Catholic Thought* (Naples, FL: Sapientia Press, 2008).

> In theological enquiry, historicism tends to appear for the most part under the guise of "modernism." Rightly concerned to make theological discourse relevant and understandable to our time, some theologians use only the most recent opinions and philosophical language, ignoring the critical evaluation which ought to be made of them in the light of the tradition. By exchanging relevance for truth, this form of modernism shows itself incapable of satisfying the demands of truth to which theology is called to respond.[26]

It would seem not too implausible. In fact, Garrigou-Lagrange's theological style provides the reference point for all authentic inquiry into the things of God, whether Thomist or not.

---

26. *Fides et ratio*, no. 87.

10

The Actuality of Aquinas and His Commentators

After the Second Vatican Council

In 1974, to commemorate the seven hundredth anniversary of the death of Thomas Aquinas, Pope Paul VI (d. 1978) sent an official "Letter" to the master of the Dominican Order, Vincent de Couesnongle.[1] Because of the theological pluralism that emerged after the Second Vatican Council, the papal notice took on a special significance. In fact, Pope Paul VI himself had let it be known, shortly after his election, that while he respected Aquinas he also liked the thought of Saint Augustine. In his "Letter," however, the pope acknowledges that his predecessors had repeatedly encouraged the study of Saint Thomas Aquinas, though he stipulated that his present recommendation also flows from his own profitable study of Saint Thomas and from his experience as a university chaplain. The pope testifies that he personally discovered "the power of [Aquinas's] teaching to persuade and form the minds of students, especially the younger ones."[2] Then the pope turned

---

1. *Lumen Ecclesiae*, "Apostolic Letter of Pope Paul VI to the Rev. Vincent De Couesnongle, Master General of the Dominican Order Marking the 7th Centenary of the Death of St Thomas Aquinas, dated 20 November 1974," *The Pope Speaks* 19 (1975): 287–307.
2. Paul VI, *Lumen Ecclesiae*, no. 2. Pope Paul VI refers to the encouragement given by an earlier encyclical of Pope Pius XI promulgated on 29 June 1923, *Studiorum Ducem*, On St. Thomas Aquinas.

his attention to admonish the anti-Thomist effect that had sprung wildly into the open after the close of the Second Vatican Council. Put otherwise, the pope acknowledged that not only did "other modes of philosophical speculation"—to borrow an expression from *Fides et ratio*—develop throughout the twentieth century but also that there arose inimical attitudes toward Aquinas and his commentators. These negative reactions toward Aquinas evolved even though, as Pope Leo XIII's enactments made clear, Thomists had rescued the church from the hodgepodge of post-Enlightenment apologetics and other threats to revealed religion.

When popes give voice to criticisms of movements afoot within the church, the admonition does not constitute an ecclesiastical meddling in academic quarrels. Popes exercise discernment as a service to the truth.[3] Here is how Pope Paul VI described the state of affairs in 1974:

> We are aware that not all of our contemporaries share Our view [about Aquinas]. But We know too that their distrust or repugnance is often due to a superficial and casual acquaintance with his teaching; in fact, at times those who reject him have not even read and studied his works. Therefore, like Pius XI, We urge all who wish to form a mature judgement in this matter: 'Go to Thomas' [citing *Studiorum Ducem*]! Obtain and read his works, not simply to find safe nourishment in his rich intellectual treasures but also, and especially, to gain a personal grasp of the sublimity, abundance and importance of the doctrine contained therein.[4]

Lumen Ecclesiae gave encouragement not only to Dominicans but also to a cadre of other clerical and lay professors who had sustained through the post-World War II period the Leonine impulse given to the study of Aquinas and the Thomist tradition.

Some outstanding examples that adorn the ranks of twentieth-century Thomist commentators include the Swiss seminary professor and cardinal Charles Journet (d. 1975); the Dominican priest and longtime Angelicum professor Angelus Walz (d. 1978), whose historical work contributed much to our knowledge about Aquinas's biography; the renowned Étienne Gilson (d. 1978), whose work at the Pontifical Institute of Mediaeval Studies in Toronto benefitted many students of Aquinas; the Alsatian Dominican Louis-Bertrand Geiger (d. 1983), who taught philosophy at Fribourg in Switzerland; and Father James A.

---

3. For a treatment of the magisterium's intervention in philosophical matters, see *Fides et ratio*, nos. 49–56.
4. Paul VI, *Lumen Ecclesiae*, no 3.

Weisheipl (d. 1984), who sustained a reading of Aquinas that highlights the importance that the philosophy of nature holds in Thomist metaphysical thought.[5] The list continues with other influential figures of the twentieth-century Thomist commentatorial tradition, such as J. H. Walgrave (d. 1986), Norbert Luyten (d. 1986), M.-M. Labourdette (d. 1990), and Josef Pieper (d. 1997). Each in his own way encouraged his students to fulfill the injunction that Pope Pius XI had expressed emphatically by making reference to a biblical allusion (see Gen 41:55), namely, "Go to Thomas!"

Expansion and Diversity

Even before the close of the Second Vatican Council, philosophical investigations and historical hermeneutics began to create differentiations among philosophers associated with Thomist studies. One author who wrote in the mid-1960s distinguished three main divisions: advocates of "Christian Philosophy," who, on this account, include Garrigou-Lagrange, Maritain, and Gilson; authors for whom "participation" serves as a leitmotif for interpreting Aquinas's philosophy, notably Cornelio Fabro (d. 1955); and those thinkers who took inspiration from the work of the Jesuit philosopher and psychologist Joseph Maréchal (d. 1944), including the Jesuit theologian Karl Rahner (d. 1984).[6] Each of these authors represents a different kind of Thomist engagement with modern philosophy. During the last three decades of the twentieth century, it became fashionable in many quarters, even among Dominicans, to enthuse over these developments and even to consider such engagements necessary in order to preserve Thomist thought from a ghetto-like confinement. By the first quarter of the twenty-first century, however, such enthusiasm seems difficult to sustain. Without gainsaying the intellectual accomplishments of men like Fabro, Maréchal, and Rahner—to mention only those thinkers most self-consciously given over to *engagement*—one may pose the question whether or not their work still commands the attention of Thomists, save those interested in historical studies. During the twentieth century, styles of Thomism began to multiply. One connoisseur identifies

---

5. For further information, see Benedict M. Ashley, "The River Forest School and the Philosophy of Nature Today," in *Philosophy and the God of Abraham: Essays in Memory of James A. Weisheipl, OP*, ed. R. James Long (Toronto: Pontifical Institute of Mediaeval Studies, 1991), 1–15.
6. For further information, see Helen James John, *The Thomist Spectrum* (New York: Fordham University Press, 1966). This author's philosophical judgments reflect a sympathy for what she calls "the critical problem of modern philosophy" (ibid., 3).

at least eight varieties of Thomist metaphysics influenced by the major philosophical movements of the period.[7] Today, however, scholars wonder whether the imperative to make Saint Thomas resemble Martin Heidegger enjoys as much support as it did during the waning decades of the twentieth century.[8]

Some studies of Aquinas and his philosophy allow the Angelic Doctor to speak for himself. A new generation of scholars has set about to expound once again the philosophy of Aquinas. They show the rightness of the conviction, that one can reconstruct "the kind of metaphysical book that [Aquinas] might have written had he chosen to do so, in accord with the philosophical order and methodology as he himself defines this."[9] And to support this conviction, there remains the witness and past lessons of some giants in the field of Thomist studies, especially the late specialists in philosophy—Vernon J. Bourke (d. 1998), Ralph McInerny (d. 2010), and William A. Wallace, OP (d. 2015)—who continued the work of the Albertus Magnus Lyceum for Natural Science, located between 1950 and 1969 in Chicago. Other scholars—perhaps to escape the competing claims about which philosophical method for interpreting Aquinas best suits contemporary vogues—have emphasized Saint Thomas the theologian or even the spiritual master.[10] The French scholar and Dominican Jean-Pierre Torrell has brought to the fore the spiritual dimension of Aquinas's works. "The very clarity," writes Torrell about Saint Thomas, "of his intellectual, philosophical, and theological commitments is immediately reflected in a religious attitude that has no equivalent except that of a mystic wholly consumed by love of the absolute."[11] In addition to Thomist philosophers and Thomist theologians, there are those who devote themselves to the development of the historical-textual approach to the life and works of Aquinas and, though to a much lesser degree than that devoted to the master himself, to those of his commentators.

It is fair to estimate that the attention paid to Thomist thought by

---

7. Benedict M. Ashley (*The Way toward Wisdom: An Interdisciplinary and Intercultural Introduction to Metaphysics* [Notre Dame: University of Notre Dame Press, 2006], 44–54), briefly describes at least eight labels used to identify different readings of Aquinas's metaphysics.
8. See Stephen L. Brock, *The Philosophy of Saint Thomas Aquinas: A Sketch* (Eugene, OR: Cascade Books, 2015), xviii.
9. John F. Wippel, *The Metaphysical Thought of Thomas Aquinas: From Finite Being to Uncreated Being* (Washington, DC: Catholic University Press of America, 2000), 594.
10. For instance, Jean-Pierre Torrell, *Aquinas's Summa: Background, Structure, and Reception* (Washington, DC: Catholic University of America Press, 2005), 133.
11. Jean-Pierre Torrell, *Saint Thomas Aquinas*, vol. 2, *Spiritual Master*, trans. Robert Royal (Washington, DC: Catholic University of America Press, 2003), viii.

scholars and institutions ranks quantitatively below what would have been the case before 1965. On the other hand, contemporary connoisseurs of Aquinas find themselves motivated by a desire to acquire as much understanding as possible about what the common doctor has to teach us. These scholars enjoy access to the tools and research necessary to pursue their research. They also possess electronic means of communication that put studies and texts at the disposal of more people than nineteenth-century classrooms and libraries would have succeeded in reaching. What is most important, Aquinas remains the Catholic theologian. After Saint Augustine, the *Catechism of the Catholic Church* refers more times to Thomas Aquinas than to any other personal authority in the Christian tradition.

Perennial Features of Thomist Thought

In the last decade of the twentieth century, Dominican Georges Cottier (d. 2016), later a Roman cardinal, gave a description of what he called, in French, the "actualité" of Thomist thought. Saint Thomas Aquinas, Cottier affirmed, has bequeathed to his students and disciples a "doctrinal, philosophical, and theological heritage of incomparable vigor and capacity for development."[12] Cottier continues to enumerate four qualities of Thomist method that persuade one to consider its perennial vitality: confidence in reason, the courage of the truth, the truth of things, and wisdom. In his discussion of these qualities, the Swiss author, who taught modern philosophy for many years at the University of Fribourg, notes how Thomist thought provides a balm for the intellectual missteps committed by many thinkers of the modern period. The abovementioned four qualities provide guidance for the one who would learn from the Thomist tradition.

Confidence in Reason

Aquinas and his authentic interpreters teach us to repose confidence in the exercise of human reason and in its capacity for embracing truth. At the same time, Aquinas reminds his readers that human reason finds itself situated on the lowest rung of created intelligences. The intelligence of angels works more quickly and efficiently than does human intelligence. We search for the one in the many, whereas angels see

---

12. Georges Cottier, "Thomisme et modernité," in *Saint Thomas au XXe siècle*, ed. Serge-Thomas Bonino (Paris: Éditions Saint-Paul, 1994), 358.

the many in the one.¹³ Still, "human intelligence," as Benedict Ashley observes, "is open to all truth, [though it] is the weakest of all existing kinds of intelligence. Because it depends for all its information on its body, its power to explore the universe and its First Cause is modest indeed."¹⁴ Modest, perhaps, but human intelligence finds itself both caused and ordered toward that which transcends it. The Thomist places confidence in reason and its ability to grasp the nature of things, "things" Aquinas carefully lays out for his followers in questions 44 through 119 of the first part of his *Summa theologiae*, where he treats the production of creatures, the distinctions among them, and their conservation in being and divine governance.¹⁵

Courage of the Truth

Confidence in the capacity of human intelligence to grasp the truth of things evolves into the characteristically Thomist posture that Cottier calls the "courage of truth."¹⁶ Indeed, the church itself has acknowledged that Saint Thomas "possessed supremely the courage of the truth."¹⁷ In his own academic career in Paris, Aquinas provides a model of what it means for a Christian thinker to engage others with the courage of truth. As the early negative reactions, even from ecclesiastical authorities, to Aquinas's teaching indicate, the man who practices courage of the truth does not always avoid conflict and misunderstanding. The authentically wise person proceeds, however, with a confidence that arises from the human intellect's capacity to discover the truth about things. The question may arise about how one may distinguish an authentic confidence in the truth from a precipitous, and sometimes defensive, rush to pronounce judgment on every philosophical and theological question. One could propose that to share in the authentic spirit of Saint Thomas requires the exercise of a rigorous critical discernment. A simpler way, though one that requires a contemplative assimilation of wisdom, is exemplified in leading North American Thomist Charles de Koninck's (1906–1965) *Ego Sapientia*.¹⁸ He

---

13. For further information, see Serge-Thomas Bonino, *Angels and Demons: A Catholic Introduction*, trans. Michael J. Miller (Washington, DC: Catholic University of America, 2016), 148–51.
14. Ashley, *Way toward Wisdom*, 276.
15. For further reflection, see Albert Patfoort, *Thomas d'Aquin: Les clés d'une théologie* (Paris: FAC-éditions, 1983), 62–70.
16. Cottier, "Thomisme," 358.
17. See *Fides et ratio*, no. 43, which cites Pope Paul VI, *Lumen Ecclesiae*, no. 8.
18. Charles de Koninck, *Ego Sapientia . . . La sagesse qui est Marie* (Montreal: Éditions de l'Université Laval, 1943).

provides an exercise in contemplative assimilation of wisdom by his presentation of the allegorical interpretations of the Book of Wisdom that center on the person of the Blessed Virgin Mary.

The Truth of Things

The phrase "veritas rerum" comes from a late work of Aquinas, the *Exposition of Aristotle's Treatise on the Heavens*.[19] Thomists commit themselves to move beyond the debate about what different people think about things to embrace the truth about things. The modern penchant for endless dialectic impairs the practice of a philosophy of "what is," to cite *Fides et ratio*.[20] On the other hand, Aquinas's serene confidence in the power of reason to grasp the essence of things derives from his trust in God the Creator. The Angelic Doctor does not hesitate to speak of the Holy Spirit as a guarantor of all truth: "Every truth, by whomever it may be said, is from the Holy Spirit in the sense that he imparts the natural light and that he moves the mind to understand and utter truth."[21] This confidence in truth explains the largesse of spirit that should characterize those who follow Aquinas. Every parcel of truth counts; though in the end, only the whole truth has grace.

Wisdom

Thomist largesse of spirit cannot coexist with a predilection for eclecticism or settling for half-truths. Aquinas wields the sword of distinction in such a way that the smallest errors in the pursuit of wisdom are exposed and discarded. No one can read Aquinas or his commentators and conclude that wisdom—doctrinal, philosophical, or theological—allows for an accommodation with error, still less for the construction of an errant syncretism. For all this, however, Aquinas never can serve as a patron saint for the denouncer, the hypercritical, or the naysayer. On the contrary, he speaks about wisdom as causing delight: "the delight of contemplating Wisdom has within itself the cause of delight."[22] An authentic embodiment of what Aquinas teaches creates in true Thomists a delightful and generous spirit. They understand that

---

19. *Sententia super librum De caelo et mundo / Exposition of Aristotle's Treatise on the Heavens*, trans. Fabian R. Larcher and Pierre H. Conway (Columbus, OH: College of St. Mary of the Springs, 1964), bk. 1, lect. 22: "the study of philosophy aims not at knowing what men feel, but at what is the truth of things."
20. *Fides et ratio*, no. 44. Nos. 43 and 44 of the encyclical explicate the uniqueness of the Thomist project.
21. *Summa theologiae* 2a–2ae, q. 109, art. 1, ad 1.

a wise exposition of truth persuades and that truth speaks for itself, even playfully. In his *Exposition of the "On the Hebdomads" of Boethius*, Aquinas, in fact, takes his clue from the book of Proverbs.

> And therefore divine Wisdom compares her delight to play. In Proverbs VIII[:30]: "I was delighted every day playing before Him," so that through the different "days" the consideration of different truths might be understood. Hence there is also added: *and there work out your conceptions*, through which, namely, a human being grasps the knowledge of truth.[23]

Perhaps more than any other explanation, Aquinas's delightful commitment to "the knowledge of truth" explains why his commentatorial tradition has survived for more than seven centuries and will continue to make Saint Thomas Aquinas an enduring influence on both philosophy and Christian theology.

---

22. Thomas Aquinas, *An Exposition of the "On the Hebdomads" of Boethius*, trans. Janice L. Schultz and Edward A. Synan (Washington, DC: Catholic University of America, 2001), ch. 1, p. 5.
23. Ibid.

Select Bibliography

Note

The life and teaching of Saint Thomas Aquinas inspires many philosophers and theologians. However, the following bibliography does not comprise an exhaustive listing of each and every work relevant to Thomas Aquinas or the Thomists. Rather, this bibliography offers only a select listing of English texts useful for readers who wish to study further the life and thought of the major figures treated in this book. The first volume of Jean-Pierre Torrell's *Saint Thomas Aquinas* contains the most recent catalogue of works by and attributed to Aquinas.

Thomas Aquinas

Aquinas, Thomas. *Thomas Aquinas: Selected Writings*. Edited and translated by Ralph McInerny. New York: Penguin Books, 1998.

Ashley, Benedict M. *The Dominicans*. Collegeville, MN: Liturgical Press, 1990.

Bauerschmidt, Frederick Christian. *Holy Teaching: Introducing the* Summa Theologiae *of St. Thomas Aquinas*. Grand Rapids: Brazos, 2005.

Boland, Vivian. *St. Thomas Aquinas*. London: Bloomsbury, 2007.

Bourke, Vernon J. *Aquinas' Search for Wisdom*. Milwaukee, WI: Bruce Publishing, 1965.

Boyle, John F. *Master Thomas Aquinas and the Fullness of Life*. South Bend, IN: St. Augustine's Press, 2014.

Brock, Stephen L. *The Philosophy of Saint Thomas Aquinas: A Sketch*. Eugene, OR: Cascade Books, 2015.

Chenu, M.-D. *Toward Understanding Saint Thomas*. Translated by A. M. Landry and D. Hughes. Chicago: Henry Regnery Publishing, 1964.

Chesterton, G. K. *Saint Thomas Aquinas*. San Francisco: Ignatius Press, 2002.

Dauphinais, Michael, and Matthew Levering. *Knowing the Love of Christ: An Introduction to the Theology of St. Thomas Aquinas*. Notre Dame: University of Notre Dame Press, 2002.

Davies, Brian. *Thomas Aquinas's* Summa contra Gentiles: *A Guide and Commentary*. New York: Oxford University Press, 2016.

———. *Thomas Aquinas's* Summa theologiae: *A Guide and Commentary*. New York: Oxford University Press, 2014.

Feser, Edward. *Aquinas: A Beginner's Guide*. Oxford: Oneworld, 2009.

Foster, Kenelm, ed. *The Life of Saint Thomas Aquinas: Biographical Documents*. Baltimore: Helicon Press, 1959.

Gilson, Étienne. *History of Christian Philosophy in the Middle Ages*. New York: Random House, 1955.

Grabmann, Martin. *The Interior Life of St. Thomas Aquinas: Presented from His Works and the Acts of His Canonization Process*. Translated by Nicholas Ashenbrener. Milwaukee, WI: Bruce Publishing, 1951.

Hinnebusch, William A. *The Dominicans: A Short History*. New York: Alba House, 1975.

———. *The History of the Dominican Order*. Vol. 1, *Origins and Growth to 1500*. New York: Alba House, 1965.

———. *The History of the Dominican Order*. Vol. 2, *The Intellectual and Cultural Life to 1500*. New York: Alba House, 1973.

Leinsle, Ulrich G. *Introduction to Scholastic Theology*. Translated by Michael J. Miller. Washington, DC: Catholic University of America Press, 2010.

Maritain, Jacques. *St. Thomas Aquinas*. New York: Meridian Books, 1958.

Maurer, Armand A. *Medieval Philosophy: A History of Philosophy*. New York: Random House, 1962.

McInerny, Ralph. *St. Thomas Aquinas*. Notre Dame: University of Notre Dame Press, 1982.

Pieper, Josef. *Guide to Thomas Aquinas*. San Francisco: Ignatius Press, 1991.

Porro, Pasquale. *Thomas Aquinas: A Historical and Philosophical Profile*. Translated by Joseph G. Trabbic and Roger W. Nutt. Washington, DC: Catholic University of America Press, 2016.

Sertillanges, A. D. *Saint Thomas Aquinas and His Work*. London: Burns, Oates & Washbourne, 1933.

Torrell, Jean-Pierre. *Saint Thomas Aquinas*. Vol. 1, *The Person and His Work*. Translated by Robert Royal. Rev. ed. Washington, DC: Catholic University of America Press, 2005.

———. *Saint Thomas Aquinas*. Vol. 2, *Spiritual Master*. Translated by Robert Royal. Washington, DC: Catholic University of America Press, 2003.

Weisheipl, James A. *Friar Thomas D'Aquino: His Life, Thought, and Works*. Washington, DC: Catholic University Press, 1983.

Thomists

Ashley, Benedict M. *Theologies of the Body: Humanist and Christian*. Braintree, MA: The Pope John Center, 1985.

_____. *The Way toward Wisdom: An Interdisciplinary and Intercultural Introduction to Metaphysics*. Notre Dame: University of Notre Dame Press, 2006.

Bedouelle, Guy. *The History of the Church*. London: Continuum, 2003.

_____. *The Reform of Catholicism: 1480-1620*. Translated by James K. Farge. Toronto: Pontifical Institute of Medieval Studies, 2008.

Cajetan, Tommaso de Vio. *Cajetan Responds: A Reader in Reformation Controversy*. Edited and translated by Jared Wicks. Washington, DC: Catholic University of America Press, 1978.

_____. *Commentary on St. Thomas Aquinas' On Being and Essence*. Translated by Lottie Kendzierski and Francis C. Wade. Milwaukee, WI: Marquette University Press, 1964.

Capreolus, John. *On the Virtues*. Edited and translated by Kevin White and Romanus Cessario. Washington, DC: Catholic University of America Press, 2001.

Cessario, Romanus. *A Short History of Thomism*. Washington, DC: Catholic University of America Press, 2005.

Doolan, Aegidius. *The Revival of Thomism*. Dublin: Clonmore & Reynolds, 1951.

Feingold, Lawrence. *The Natural Desire to See God According to St. Thomas Aquinas and His Interpreters*. 2nd ed. Ave Maria, FL: Sapientia Press, 2010.

Feser, Edward. *Scholastic Metaphysics: A Contemporary Introduction*. Heusenstamm: Editiones Scholasticae, 2014.

Garrigou-Lagrange, Reginald. *Reality: A Synthesis of Thomistic Thought*. Translated by Patrick Cummins. St. Louis: Herder, 1950.

Horst, Ulrich. *The Dominicans and the Pope: Papal Teaching Authority in the Medieval and Early Modern Thomist Tradition*. Translated by James D. Mixson. Notre Dame: University of Notre Dame Press, 2006.

John, Helen James. *The Thomist Spectrum*. New York: Fordham University Press, 1966.

John of St. Thomas. *The Gifts of the Holy Spirit*. Translated by Dominic Hughes. New York: Sheed & Ward, 1951.

_____. *Introduction to the* Summa theologiae *of Thomas Aquinas*. Translated by Ralph McInerny. South Bend, IN: St. Augustine's Press, 2004.

_____. *The Material Logic of John of St. Thomas: Basic Treatises*. Translated by Yves

R. Simon, John J. Glanville, and G. Donald Hollenhorst. Chicago: University of Chicago Press, 1955.

———. *Outlines of Formal Logic*. Translated by Francis C. Wade. Milwaukee, WI: Marquette University Press, 1955.

Kennedy, Leonard A. *A Catalogue of Thomists: 1270–1900*. Houston: Center for Thomistic Studies, 1987.

Kerr, Fergus. *After Aquinas: Versions of Thomism*. Oxford: Blackwell, 2002.

Long, Steven A. *Analogia Entis: On the Analogy of Being, Metaphysics, and the Act of Faith*. Notre Dame: University of Notre Dame Press, 2011.

———. *Natura Pura: On the Recovery of Nature in the Doctrine of Grace*. New York: Fordham University Press, 2010.

Matava, R. J. *Divine Causality and Human Free Choice: Domingo Báñez, Physical Premotion and the Controversy de Auxiliis Revisited*. Leiden: Brill, 2016

McInerny, Ralph. *Praeambula Fidei: Thomism and the God of the Philosophers*. Washington, DC: Catholic University of America Press, 2006.

McLean, George F., ed. *Teaching Thomism Today*. Washington, DC: Catholic University of America Press, 1963.

Nichols, Aidan. *Reason with Piety: Garrigou-Lagrange in the Service of Catholic Thought*. Naples, FL: Sapientia Press, 2008.

Roensch, Frederick J. *Early Thomistic School*. Dubuque, IA: Priory Press, 1964.

Torrell, Jean-Pierre. *Aquinas's Summa: Background, Structure, and Reception*. Translated by Benedict M. Guevin. Washington, DC: Catholic University of America Press, 2005.

Index

Abelard, Peter, 32, 69
act and potency, xiii, 12, 52
Aeterni Patris xi, 19n1, 121n33, 124n5, 127–29
Agramunt, Vincent Ferrer, 113
Akindynos, Gregory, 59
Albert the Great, 6–8, 21, 24n14, 85
Alexander, Noël (Natalis), 117
Ambrose of Milan, xi
Ancina, Juvenal, 102
Anselm of Canterbury, 21–22
Antoninus of Florence, 74,
Aristotle, xiii, 13, 24, 30, 33–36, 41–42, 49–50, 73, 82, 86, 139
Ashley, Benedict M., 16n42, 81n17, 90n38, 107, 153n5, 136n7, 138
Augustine, xi, xiv, 4, 33, 49, 99, 116, 137
Augustinians, 50–51, 59, 85–86, 102, 119
Aureolus, Peter, 73
Averroes, 34, 41

Babenstuber, Ludwig, 108
Báñez, Dominic, xvii, 89, 100–102, 105, 108, 114
Bartholomew of Capua, 54
Bartholomew of Lucca, 64

Bartholomew of Medina, 97–98
Beatitudes, 96
Bedouelle, Guy, 3n2, 32n35, 71n21, 72n23, 73n26, 75n31, 81n14, 91n40, 96n9, 110n4, 120n28, 129n16
Benedict (Saint), 4, 15
Benedict XIII, 106, 119–20
Benedict XVI, 32
Bernard of Clairvaux, 8, 32
Billuart, Charles René, 115–17
Black Death plague, 60, 64
Bloy, Léon, 130
Boethius, 22, 34, 60, 140
Bonaventure, xi, 42, 52n16
Bongean, Bernard (Bonjoannes), 86n30
Bonino, Serge-Thomas, 73n27, 137n12, 138n13
Borgia, Francis, 86
Bossuet, Jacques-Bénigne, 109
Bourke, Vernon J., 136
Boxadors, John Thomas de, 118–19, 124
Boyle, John F., 34n44,
Boyle, Leonard E., 121, 124n5, 127n8
Brague, Rémi, 34n45
Buzzetti, Vincent Benedict, 121, 124

145

Caetano, Joseph, 111–12
Cajetan, Thomas de Vio, xi, xvii, 77n2, 79–84, 89, 102
Calvinism, 96, 99
Cambridge, University of, 90
Cano, Melchior, 89
Capreolus, John, 9, 71–74, 78, 80–81, 83–85, 105, 106
Carletti, Angelo, 68
Carmelites, 86, 100, 102–4, 114
Carranza, Bartholomew, 88, 90
Cartesians. *See* Descartes
Cassiodorus, 60
casuistry/casuist, 96–98, 112, 113, 119
Catherine of Siena, xvii, 64–65, 80, 111, 126
Catharinus, Ambrosius, 82, 88, 99
Chalcedon, Council of, 66n8
Charronelle, Gilles, 78n5
Chenu, M.-D., 8n14, 9n19, 15, 22, 32n36
Chesterton, G. K., 16, 26, 34
Cicero, 33
Cistercians, 39–40, 102, 119
clergy/clerics, xvi, 6, 15–16, 27, 28, 32, 59, 67–68, 81, 86, 90, 95, 115, 118–19, 120, 134
Columbus, Christopher, 83
commentators/commentatorial tradition. *See* Thomist commentatorial tradition
Complutenses, 103
conciliarism/conciliarist, 66
Condillac, Étienne Bonnot de, 121
connaturality, 114
contemplation, 5, 12, 72
Contenson, Vincent, 106, 115
Cottier, Georges, 137, 138
Couesnongle, Vincent de, 133

creed, 31, 54, 66n8
Crockaert, Peter, 77–78, 83–84
curriculum, theological/philosophical, 78, 88

Dante, 42
De Auxiliis controversy, 101
De Franceschi, Sylvio Hermann, 116n19, 120n26
Dechamps, Étienne, 98n14
Descartes, René, 93–94, 104, 109, 123, 125
Deza, Diego de, 83
Di Noia, J. A., 129n18
dialecticism/dialectic/dialecticians, 26, 57, 72, 85–86, 139
disputatio/disputation, 14, 35–36, 103, 117
Dominic (Saint), 4–5, 10, 16–17, 47, 111
Dominic of Flanders, 73–74
Dominicans, 3–4, 9–13, 15, 17, 22, 26–27, 31, 33, 36–43, 51–59, 64, 66–67, 69–70, 72–74, 77–80, 85–94, 101–2, 104, 107, 111, 116, 118–20, 126–29, 134–35
Dominici, John, 74
Doré, Pierre, 95n7
Dungersheim, Jerome, 85
Durand, Bartélemy, 69
Durandus of Saint-Pourçain, xvii, 56–58, 72

Eckhart, John, 65
eclecticism/eclectic, xvii, 73–74, 81, 95, 105, 107, 114
Eco, Umberto, 64
Education, 5, 6, 14, 31–32, 79, 102
Edward I, 50
Edward III, 60

INDEX

Emery, Gilles, 8n18
encyclicals, papal, 19, 21, 127–29
epistemology, 93, 123
essence and existence, xiii, 12, 121
evangelization, xvi, 81, 95
existence and essence. *See* essence and existence

Fabro, Cornelio, 24n15, 105n32, 135
faith and reason, xiv, xv–xvi, 20–22, 32–34, 48, 87, 110, 124, 131
Ferrariensis (Francis Silvestri of Ferrara), 82–83
fideism, 110
Fides et ratio, xiin3, xivn8, 21n8, 34n40, 48n6, 93n3, 128n10, 132n26, 134, 138–39
form and matter, xiii, 41–42, 52
France, 17, 31, 39, 48, 57, 58, 60–61, 63, 64, 72, 73, 82, 87, 94–96, 113, 114, 115, 119, 120–21, 129, 130
Francis (Saint), 9
Francis II, 125
Franciscans, 41–42, 49–55, 57, 59–60, 64, 67–69, 73, 118
Fribourg, University of, 129, 134, 137

Gardeil, H.-D., 117n24
Garrigou-Lagrange, Reginald, 12, 130–32
Gauthier, R. A., 19–20
Gazzaniga, Peter Mary, 119
Geiger, Louis-Bertrand, 134
Ghislieri, Michael. *See* Pius V
Gilby, Thomas, 29
Gilson, Étienne, 56, 70, 93, 134, 135
Godin, William Peter, 63–64
Gonet, John Baptist, 106, 115, 117
González, Cerafino, 127

Gotti, Vincent Louis, 110–11
Goudin, Anthony, 107, 115
Grabmann, Martin, 4, 21
grace, xiv, 11, 22, 29, 67, 71, 88, 90, 99–102, 107, 112, 114, 116, 121, 139
Grasset, Jean, 107
Gregory XI, 64
Gregory XVI, 124
Grignion de Montfort, Louis Mary, 107
Grosseteste, Robert, xi
Gui, Bernard, 64
Günther, Anton, 124–25, 127

happiness, 30, 113–14
Hegelianism, 124
Heidegger, Martin, 136
Henry of Ghent, xi, 73
Henry Suso, 65
heresy, 49–50, 54, 56, 64
Hermes, George, 124–25, 127
Hinnebusch, William A., 77n2, 79n9, 91
historicism, 132
Hothum, William, 50, 63
Hugh of Saint-Victor, xi,
humanism/humanists, 72–74, 79, 85–86, 87, 89, 112
Hume, David, 109

Ignatius of Antioch, xi
Ignatius of Loyola, 88, 94
Immaculate Conception, 67–68, 71
infallibilists, 66
Inquisition, 64, 88, 101
instrumentality, 27, 35, 89, 90, 100
intellect, xii–xiii, 12, 34–36, 63, 138
Irenaeus of Lyons, xi

147

Jacobins, 40, 48
Jansen, Cornelius, 106
Jansenism, 21, 106–7, 116
Jesuits, 86, 94–95, 98, 100–102, 105, 107, 118, 121, 124–25, 126, 127, 129, 135
John XXII, 40, 55, 57–59, 66
John of Montesono, 67
John of St. Thomas (John Poinsot), 94, 104–5
John Paul II (Karol Wojtyła), 21, 127–28, 131
Journet, Charles, 134
Justin Martyr, 20

Kantianism, 124
Kilwardby, Robert, 41
Kleutgen, Joseph, 127
Knapwell, Richard, 50–51
Köllin, Conrad, 84–85
Koninck, Charles de, 25n19, 138–39
Kydones, Demetrios, 59
Kydones, Prochoros, 59

Labourdette, M.-M., 135
Lacordaire, Henri-Dominic, 120
Lamennais, Félicité Robert de, 142
laxism, 97–98
Leibniz, Gottfried Wilhelm, 117
Leo XIII, xi, 125, 126–27, 128–29, 131, 134
Leonine Period / Renewal, 127, 126–27, 128–29, 134
Liberatore, Matthew, 125
Liguori, Alphonsus, 112
Locke, John, 109, 121
Lombard, Peter, 9, 28, 68, 78
Long, Steven A., 21n6, 82n19, 100n17, 101–2, 107n40
Louis IV (the Bavarian), 57

Louis IX, 4, 15, 32
Louis XIV, 96, 107
Louvain, University of, 78, 104, 119
Luther, Martin, 68–69, 80, 82, 85, 93, 95
Luyten, Norbert, 135

Macclesfield, William, 52
MacIntyre, Alasdair, 14
Major, John, 77
Mandonnet, Pierre, 26n22, 83n23, 101n23, 116n20
manuals, 66, 102–3, 121, 125
Maréchal, Joseph, 135
Maritain, Jacques, 93, 105, 130, 135
Maritain, Raïssa, 130
Marquis of Pombal, 118
Martinez de Ripalda, Juan, 9
Mary. *See* Immaculate Conception
Masdeu brothers, 121
Massoulié, Antoninus, 113–15
matter and form. *See* form and matter
Maurer, Armand A., 22, 52n16, 69n17, 81n16
McCool, Gerald A., 117n23, 124n2, 126n7
McInerny, Ralph M., 82n18, 83n22, 136
Medici, Lorenzo de', 73–74
Melanchthon, Philip, 85–86
mendicant orders, 3, 9, 15–16, 35–36, 42, 50, 53, 58, 59, 86, 102
Mercedarians, 102
metaphysics, xii, 30, 42, 50, 69, 83, 100, 102, 105, 119, 136
missionaries, 5, 91
modernism/modernists, 131–32
Molina, Luis de, xvii, 100–107
monasticism, 4, 5, 7, 13, 15, 32, 78

monopsychism, 34–35
Monson, John de, 71
Montecassino, Abbey of, 4, 7, 13
moral theology, 27, 29, 68, 74, 80, 96–98, 99, 103–4, 106, 112–15, 117
moralism, 119
Mozart, Wolfgang Amadeus, 118
Murray, Paul, 26n19

Nadal, Jerome, 94
Napoleon, 120
Natalis, Hervaeus, 57–58
natural philosophy/physics, 34, 102, 135, 136
nature, xiv, 11, 22, 51, 99, 101–2, 138
neo-Thomism, 129
Newman, John Henry, 24, 68
Nicholas III, 49, 54, 56, 57–58
Nicholas IV, 16n42, 51
Nichols, Aidan, 131n25
nominalism, 69

Ockhamism, 59–60, 69–70
Olivi, Peter John, 53, 54
ontologism, 21
Orford, Robert, 51
original sin. *See* sin
orthodoxy, 22, 49, 64, 110
Oxford, University of, 41–43, 48, 50, 51, 87, 90, 116

Padua, 68, 81n17, 107
Palamism, 59
papacy, 23–24, 54, 59, 64, 66, 111
Paris, University of, 3, 6, 9, 15–17, 19, 22, 23, 26, 27, 32–33, 35, 36, 37, 39–43, 48, 49, 50, 52, 56, 60, 64, 67, 68, 71–72, 77, 83, 84, 88, 138

participation, 135
Pasnau, Robert, 13n34, 33n39
patristics, 24, 33
Patuzzi, John Vincent, 112–13
Pecham, John, 41, 49–50, 54
Pergolesi, John Baptist, 110
person/personhood, xiv, 42, 57, 98, 99–100
Peter of Ailly, 71–72
Peter of Auvergne, 59
Peter of Bergamo, 74
Peter of Palude, 58
Philip IV (king of Spain), 104
Philip VI (king of France), 60
philosophy, xi, xiv, xvi, 20–21, 22, 34, 48, 69, 70, 74, 79, 83, 102, 105, 117, 123–32, 135–36, 139
Piccardi, Seraphino, 107
Pico della Mirandola, Giovanni, 74, 97
Pieper, Josef, 48, 60n33, 69, 70n18, 135
Pinckaers, Servais, 96n10
Piny, Alexander, 106
Pius IV, 89–90
Pius V, 78, 90–91
Pius VI, 119
Pius VII, 121
Pius IX, 64, 67, 124
Pius XI, 133n2, 134, 135
Planudes, Maximus, 59
Platonism/Neoplatonism, 24–25, 85n25
poetry, 25–26, 65, 99, 111
Pomponazzi, Pietro, 81
Porro, Pasquale, 30n34
potency and act. *See* act and potency
praeambula fidei, 82
preaching, 5, 14, 38, 75, 117

predestination, 99–102, 106, 107, 119
promotion, 101n20, 114
Prierias (Silvester Mazzolini), 81
Primadizzi, Rambert dei, 52
Princeps Thomistarum, 72
principles, philosophical and theological, xii–xiv, xvii, 74, 81, 93, 103
probabiliorism, 97
probabilism, 98, 106, 112
Protestantism, xvii, 86, 94–96
Pseudo-Dionysius, xi, 24
psychology, 102

Quidort, Jean, 51–52
quodlibetal, 36, 68

Rahner, Karl, 135
Ramirez, Santiago, 94n4, 105n33
rationalism, xiv, 111, 128
realism/realist, xii–xiv, 93, 131
reason and faith. *See* faith and reason
Reformation, Protestant / Protestant Reformers, xvii, 85, 86–88, 93, 117
Reginald of Piperno, 31, 38
Rerum Novarum, 128
revolutions, 31, 39n3, 48, 109, 120, 124
Roensch, Frederick J., 49n8, 51n13, 52n17
Roscelin of Compiègne, 69
Roselli, Salvatore, 117, 118, 121, 125
Rousseau, Jean-Jacques, 93, 109, 110
Ruffi, Conrad, 67
Rummel, Erika, 71n22, 72n24, 79n10, 87

sacraments, 14, 20, 25, 27, 60, 89–90, 97, 105, 110, 111
sacrifice, Eucharistic, 6
Salmanticenses, 103–4
Sanseverino, Cajetan, 125–26
Savonarola, Jerome, 74–75, 79
schism, 39, 66
scholasticism/scholastics, xi, xii, 60, 70, 86–87, 104, 106, 121, 125, 127
science, 10, 13, 14, 16, 21, 27, 48, 83, 94, 97, 110, 113, 115, 123, 127, 136
Scotism/Scotists, 64, 68–69
Scotus, John Duns, xvii, 59, 64, 67–69, 73, 105
Scripture, xvi, 8–9, 10, 112
Shakespeare, William, 3, 11n25, 60
Siger of Brabant, 35
Simon, Richard, 107
sin, 67, 99, 112–13
Soncinas, Paul Barbus, 74
Sordi, Dominic, 121, 124–25
Sordi, Serafino, 121, 124–25
Soto, Dominic de, 87–89
Soto, Peter de, 90
Spina, Bartholomew, 81
Spinoza, Baruch, 110
spirituality, 52, 65, 88
Suárez, Francis, 105
Suarezian, 121
substance, xiii, 41, 49, 52
Summa contra Gentiles, 19–21, 82–83
Summa theologiae, 5, 6, 28–30, 33, 34, 37, 38, 52, 59, 68, 77–82, 86, 90, 91, 97, 101, 103, 114, 138
Sutton, Thomas, 59

Taparelli D'Azeglio, Louis, 125
Tauler, John, 65

Tempier, Stephen, 41, 49
Teresa of Ávila, 65, 100, 102–4
Terreni, Guido, 66
Tertullian, 34
Tetzel, Johann, 95
Thomist commentatorial tradition, xv–xvi, 11, 72, 78, 80–82, 83, 84, 86, 87, 89, 91, 94–96, 101, 103, 104, 105, 107, 110, 112, 114, 115–17, 118–20, 121–22, 126, 128–32, 135
Torquemada, John de, 66
Torrell, Jean-Pierre, 4n4, 8n15, 8n16, 20n2, 25n16, 26, 28n27, 30n32, 33n38, 36n50, 40n6, 42n12, 64n2, 78, 129n15, 136, 141
Treaty of Westphalia, 87n34, 96
Trent, Council of, 66, 82, 84, 86–91, 97
Trinity, 20
truth, xii, xv–xvi, 10–13, 20, 22, 36, 48, 50–51, 65, 86, 112, 131, 132, 137–40
tutiorism, 97
Tyrrell, George, 74n29

Urban IV, 23, 25, 26
Urban V, 47, 48

Vatican Council I, 54
Vatican Council II, 40, 128, 131, 133–34, 135
virtue, 29, 31, 84, 96, 114
Vitoria, Francis de, 83–84, 88, 89

Walgrave, J. H., 135
Wallace, William A., 136
Walz, Angelo, 89–90, 134
Wars of Religion, French, 87, 95
Weisheipl, James A., 6n9, 8n16, 16n40, 24n14, 40n5, 41, 43n14, 49n7, 50n12, 53n18, 83n22, 95n6, 123, 129n14, 134–135
William de la Mare, 40, 50–52
William of Ockham, 59–60, 69–70, 72
William of Saint-Amour, 16
William of Tocco, 64
Wippel, John F., 30, 136n9
wisdom, xiii–xv, 10–13, 72, 139–40

Velázquez, Diego, 104
Voltaire, 109–10

Zigliara, Thomas Mary (Francis), 126–29

www.ingramcontent.com/pod-product-compliance
Lightning Source LLC
Chambersburg PA
CBHW071206070526
44584CB00019B/2932